CUMB

MURL
CASEBOOK

To the people of Cumbria, and in particular all those who remember the young author, once of Crindledyke Estate, Kingstown. I remember you all, wonderful times!

CUMBRIA

MURDER CASEBOOK

PAUL HARRISON

COUNTRYSIDE BOOKS
NEWBURY · BERKSHIRE

First published 1995
© Paul Harrison 1995

COUNTRYSIDE BOOKS
3 Catherine Road
Newbury, Berkshire

ISBN 1 85306 382 7

Produced through MRM Associates Ltd., Reading
Typeset by Paragon Typesetters, Queensferry
Printed by Woolnough Bookbinding, Irthlingborough

Contents

Acknowledgements

When Countryside Books approached me to research and write this work they knew full well that I would be filled with enthusiasm for the task at hand. I am by birth a Cumbrian, born and raised in Kingstown, now a suburb of Carlisle. There is always something special about writing about one's own county, and I can only hope that I have done the county justice with my small selection of the most dastardly murders to occur within its boundaries. I grew up in Rudge, Martin and Baker territory, I knew as a child all there was to know about the case. I recall the A74 being built and the carry-on there was when Archibald Hall dumped the body of one of his victims in an underground pipe beside it. As a teenager, along with my friends we would visit this pipe and dare each other to crawl through it.

Before you say it, no I was not a morbid youngster. I was inquisitive, I still am, but all I sought at the time was the truth. The tales and folklore associated with murderous acts tend to cloud issues, when fact becomes lost in fiction. This then is the first book based solely upon Cumbrian murders which is the result of dedicated research based on hard fact from extant documents, many of which have never been viewed this century.

It goes without saying that I could never have completed this work without the kind assistance of others. My appreciation goes to Sir Charles Graham Bt, for everything he supplied upon Rudge, Martin, and Baker; to the Cumbria Constabulary for their kind assistance with my research; to Dennis Perriam for allowing me to view his excellent research notes upon the Citadel site and the County gaol; and the Cumberland

Newspaper group for supplying some of the illustrations. My thanks also to the Carlisle records office at Carlisle Castle; to the staff of Carlisle City library, Workington library, Barrow library, Keswick library and Maryport library; and to the staff of the Public Records Office, Kew, where many of the old files relating to a number of these cases can be found.

To Fiona Hunter, Eric and Victoria Wilson, Christine Evans and Norman Allen I pass my sincere thanks for support and informative suggestions, especially those relating to their ancestors. A special thank you to Warwick Sloan whose interest in the Plumpton murder was a source of inspiration to me. I would also like to thank my family, Lesley, Paula and Mark Harrison for putting up with my research for all this time.

Paul Harrison
Summer 1995

1

THE OLD GAOL

The county of Cumbria, created from the ancient counties of Cumberland and Westmorland, is synonymous with picturesque beauty, epitomised by rambling hillsides with meandering streams gushing freely into lakes and tarns. Without doubt the Lake District is one of the most beautiful places on earth. Yet Cumbria, like so many other counties, has a dark and mysterious past.

Over the centuries, Cumbria has housed some vicious and hardened criminals, especially the city of Carlisle where the county gaol was situated. Murder was merely classed as one of the more serious crimes of the Middle Ages; the punishment for treason could be absurdly horrific, and similarly, common thieves would be executed. As crime became more of a problem within the county one of the major difficulties facing the early authorities was the housing of offenders prior to trial. The Assizes of Clarendon in 1166 motioned that all county sheriffs should ensure that gaols were built within their boundaries to house criminals.

Records show that prisoners were held in this county from as early as 1167, when Robert Troite, Sheriff of Cumberland, was involved in the movement of prisoners from York to Carlisle. The year 1172 saw expenditure to the amount of 53s 4d laid out for work upon the gaol of Carlisle. Initially the dungeons at Carlisle Castle were used as prison cells, but these would eventually prove unable to cope with the high number of offenders awaiting trial.

Little changed for the next 150 years, but matters were complicated with the embarrassing crime for which the Earl of Carlisle and Governor of Carlisle Castle, Sir Andrew De Harcla, was charged – high treason, no less!

De Harcla had allegedly made a treaty with the Scots, then the enemies of the English. On 2nd March 1323 Sir Galfrid de Scope arrived in the county to sit in judgment at Carlisle Castle over De Harcla. The prisoner was found guilty and sentenced to an ignominious death. He was dragged through the streets of Carlisle to Henriby (Harraby) where he was hanged, beheaded and his body divided into four quarters. These were then distributed to Bristol, Dover and Newcastle, with the fourth section remaining in Carlisle. Upon the direct instruction of Sir Galfrid, each portion was hung upon the relevant city wall in full public view as a deterrent to other would-be traitors!

The year 1378 saw the construction of what can be classed as the first county gaol. It was a purpose-built prison situated within the castle's outer gateway; built and designed by John Lewyn, it proved to be a service-able alternative to the dungeons, albeit a temporary measure. The years of use and abuse eventually proved too heavy a burden for the ancient castle structure, and by 1605 some 28 prisoners out of a total of 33 in custody escaped through inadequate security and poor structural organisation.

The Citadel site, which was situated within Carlisle city boundaries and had long since been made redundant from its original purpose as a defensive barrier, was taken over as the county gaol. A little refurbishment was required but by 1611 all prisoners were being taken to the western bastion of the Citadel, which had been transformed into the confinement area.

Once again the situation was less than practicable, as long stay prisoners suffered greatly in the squalor which surrounded them. As with the castle, parts of the Citadel had succumbed to the ravages of time. In 1645 some of it had to be knocked down as an alternative to falling down of its own accord, yet still no architectural alterations were made to the building, which was virtually ruinous and most unsuitable as a prison.

The 'Hanging Judge' George Jeffreys arrived in the county in August 1684 to preside over the assizes. He can only have been impressed by the 15 gun salute he received upon entering Carlisle city boundaries, but he subsequently demanded to see the gaol and was disgusted by what he found. He fined the governors for their apathetic ineptitude in running such a disorderly establishment. He further demanded that a new gaol be constructed as soon as was humanly possible. His trip to the county was not a happy one, especially when he heard a highly political speech made at the cathedral, the contents of which clashed with his own beliefs. The result was that two people were condemned to death!

In 1686 some property and land owned by Recorder John Aglionby, situated near the Citadel site and English Gate, was purchased by the county. The property was an outer office of one of the conventual buildings of the Blackfriars, and was claimed to have come into the possession of the Aglionbys upon the dissolution of the religious houses in the previous century. The site and property were handed over at a cost of £200. Included in the agreement was a large garden which would provide a more than adequate exercise area for the prisoners.

By 1689 the new gaol was completed and all prisoners successfully transferred. The exercise area was one of the finest in the land, so fine that it was divided in two and one half walled off and made into a bowling green for the wealthy. The prisoners were less than pleased and on one occasion, attempted to tear down the wall with their bare hands!

Prisoners were more or less expected to fend for themselves. Those with cells which fronted onto the street could beg for food, water, or even straw for a bed from passers by, but others with no such view suffered greatly, receiving old straw and stale food. The more affluent prisoners were actually allowed to leave prison on market day and purchase fruit and other provisions to make life a little more comfortable.

In 1781, gaol fever (typhus) spread through the county gaol and into the city, resulting in some 600 people becoming infected, 52 of whom died. The disease was believed to have spread from an overcrowded slum outside the prison walls, which had boarded up windows in order to avoid payment of window tax. The premises were duly burned to the ground.

A local doctor by the name of Heystrom carried out tests on infected prisoners, and claimed that two and a half bottles of port per prisoner per day would act as sufficient remedy to clear the disease. The proposal was ignored, much to the disgust of the prisoners.

In March 1807 a relatively simple escape from the prison occurred. In the early hours of the morning one of the prisoners requested some water. A turnkey brought it to him but as he entered the cell, the six prisoners inside overpowered him and escaped to another part of the gaol. Other prisoners and turnkeys were threatened at gunpoint until eventually the six got away, only to be recaptured within three hours.

September of 1808 saw another five felons escape, sawing through their restraining leg irons with a rough-edged knife. They removed the stone pavement from beneath the cell door and slid beneath it, then climbed the gaol wall to freedom. Two were recaptured, the other three were never seen again! The pavement stones were replaced in a more secure manner, with iron bars riveted across them. The masons declared that the cells were now secure. A few days later, three further prisoners escaped by removing one of the iron bars from the cell window and dislodging several of the newly laid stones. The humiliation of the authorities was complete.

One of the most horrific incidents relating to the gaol occurred on the gallows situated at the south east rooftop angle on the gaol front, on 18th September 1813. Daniel MacRory was one of several burglars sentenced to be executed. The exploits of this character had spread far and wide, and it was expected that there would be a last minute attempt to free him.

A large body of constables were in attendance, as too were a troop of the 2nd Regiment of Guards and the 7th Regiment of Foot. A huge crowd had assembled. MacRory left the gaol and climbed onto the gallows, where he asked to see the rope which was to hang him. He objected to its thickness, claiming that it was too thin to hold his weight. Playing to his audience, he bowed to the assembled throng before the noose was placed around his neck. The spectacle which followed was indeed a unique one in the history of the county gaol. As MacRory had stated, the rope was too thin, and snapped, sending him crashing to the floor of the pit beneath the gallows, breaking his leg as he did so! Officials were horrified and for a while did not know what to do. Eventually, MacRory was lifted back onto the gallows in a chair. He was in agony and his cries of pain deeply upset the crowd. The noose was again placed around his neck and this time, despite a severe snap, it held firm, sending MacRory to his death.

Catastrophe followed catastrophe. In December 1816 a turnkey was knocked to the ground as he entered a cell. His keys were stolen, he was secured in the cell and the escapees made their way to his home within the gaol.

There they forced the turnkey's wife to open the gaol gates to allow them freedom.

It was not until 1821, when a further fine was imposed upon the county for the sad state of the gaol, that matters improved. By 1823 new properties had been purchased within the direct vicinity of the Citadel site as work commenced to modernise and restructure the prison. Eventually, the old gaol dating from 1688-89 was demolished, in 1825. Two years later the county's new gaol was complete at a cost of £43,000. The new prison could house 150 prisoners, but when the Prison Act of 1865 declared that prisoners should not share cells, extensive alterations were again carried out at a cost of £16,000. The revamped gaol now had 164 individual cells, 112 for male prisoners and 52 for female; all work was completed in 1868.

Executions were not always carried out upon the gaol corner, (which still stands on the principal turret facing English Street, and is denoted by a round plaque upon the wall). Other gallows were constructed at various sites, but initially Harraby Hill, or Gallows Hill, was the official place of execution. It was here in 1746 that 30 poor souls met their maker for taking part in the Rebellion of 1745. An abhorrent sentence was passed upon those found guilty. 'You and every one of you prisoners at the bar return to the prison from whence you came, and from thence you must be drawn to the place of execution. When you come there you must be hanged by the neck – but not till you be dead; for you must be cut down alive; then your bowels must be taken out and burnt before your faces; then your heads must be severed from your bodies and your bodies each divided into four quarters. These must be at the King's disposal. And God have mercy on your souls.' One of those being sentenced was Cappock the mock Bishop, who cried out, 'We shan't be tried by a Cumberland jury in the other world.'

A further gallows site was constructed at Low Sands, just off the nearby Eden Bridge, and another was later erected between Warwick Street and Corporation Road, known as 'Hangman's Close'.

It was however the executions at the gaol which generally aroused great public sympathy. In the space of two years five men were despatched from the gallows on the gaol corner. Two of these were John Townsend, found guilty of forgery, and Christopher Gale, found guilty of robbing the mail train between Cockermouth and Maryport in 1819. Both men were sentenced to death and shared the same cell. Townsend was a father of three and his case met with great displeasure from the public who felt that he was only trying to provide for his family. The double execution was to take place in April 1819.

The men were confined to a cell which was dripping with water, overrun with vermin and had a small dirty pile of straw for both to sleep upon. Such conditions would not have caused concern had the prisoners been vicious murderers, but this pair were simple thieves. To make them spend their last days on earth like animals was not a kindly act.

There was a public outcry as people paid money to visit the pair in their cell and to witness their degraded state. On the day of execution, thousands of people packed the streets surrounding the gaol and hissed and booed as the execution was carried out. The authorities were pelted with stones and much else besides; they had lost a great deal of credibility with their treatment of Gale and Townsend.

The following year saw the execution of three dastardly criminals by the names of John Woof, William Armstrong and John Little, who had burgled a house at Soulby. The gang were masked and armed with pistols and swords. Their victims were tortured with threats and were put through a terrifying ordeal.

On this occasion public sympathy turned to anger, and the trio were put to death on the gallows to loud cheers and the applause of the assembled thousands. Shortly before being executed, Armstrong, who denied his guilt, attacked the executioner and had to be restrained by constables. The atmosphere among those present was one of great satisfaction and excitement; few sentenced prisoners received such a hostile reception for their crimes.

The following is a complete list of those persons executed at the county gaol between 1800 and the last execution to take place in the county in 1892. The last public execution was that of William Charlton in 1862, and the first to take place within the confines of the gaol, that of Dalgleish, who was tried in Manchester and brought to Carlisle for execution, his crime having taken place in Penrith. It is perhaps curious to note that no women were hanged in the last century of executions in the county.

September 1800	– A McGowan; uttering a forged note
September 1803	– J Hatfield; fraud
August 1808	– J Wood; double murder
November 1809	– J Edwards; robbery
September 1813	– D MacRory; burglary
September 1816	– J Donald; burglary
April 1819	– C Gale; theft of mail bags. Robbery
April 1819	– J Townsend; fraud
August 1820	– J Lightfoot; murder
September 1820	– J Woof; robbery
September 1820	– W Armstrong; robbery
September 1820	– J Little; robbery
March 1827	– R Fox; attempted murder
March 1827	– P Tinnaney; murder
March 1835	– J Pearson; murder
August 1847	– J Thompson; attempted murder
March 1855	– T Munroe; murder

August 1860   – G Cass; murder
March 1862   – W Charlton; murder
December 1876 – J Dalgleish; murder
February 1886 – A Rudge; murder
February 1886 – J Martin; murder
February 1886 – J Baker; murder
November 1887 – W Hunter; murder
March 1892   – J Wilson; murder.

2

WICKED JAMES WOOD

**THE MURDER OF MARGARET SMITH AND JANE PATTINSON AT
LONGBURN, JANUARY 1808**

In the Cumberland of the early 19th century, the main employment was still that of the farmer and work upon the land. However, with towns such as Maryport, Workington and Carlisle expanding, builders, carpenters and other tradespersons could also make a reasonable living. Extra income was raised by selling goods at any of the many markets in the region; particularly fine at this time was the Wigton market, where one could purchase just about anything desired.

Thomas Smith was something of an entrepreneur. In 1807 he owned a small farm at Longburn in the parish of Bromfield, which is situated close to the Solway coast and not too far from the markets at Wigton and Aspatria. Smith was a hard working man, indeed his entire family were industrious. While he worked the farm and tended to his cattle, his wife, Margaret, and her sister Jane Pattinson, who also resided at Longburn, would spend much of their time weaving, making blankets and other small items of clothing. These in turn would be sold at one of the markets, either at Wigton, Aspatria or even Maryport and Workington. So far as financial matters were concerned, the Smith family were reasonably well off, as they reaped the benefit of their hard work.

Late one afternoon in May 1807, a stranger arrived in

16

Longburn. He was seen by several people, explaining that he was in search of work in the area. He had little success until he knocked at the solid oak door of the Smiths' farmhouse. Margaret Smith answered his knock and asked what his business was. 'I am a trained weaver,' the stranger explained, 'I've come in search of work. I am fit and healthy and can turn my hand to just about any kind of work, especially farming the fields. Do you have a need for an extra pair of hands?' Margaret's husband was still away at market, but she recalled Thomas had said only a few days earlier that he could do with some help with the weaving and on the farm in general.

The stranger, who introduced himself as James Wood, was pleasant enough and was courteous and polite to Margaret Smith, who advised him that her husband was looking for someone to help out on the farm, and to wait until he returned home.

A short time later, Thomas Smith returned to Longburn. Within a few minutes Wood had been given a job, albeit nothing permanent, but the opportunity was there should he prove his worth. A rate for the job was agreed and Smith charged his new labourer seven shillings for his board.

Within a few weeks, Wood was producing so much material from his loom that on several occasions he earned 15 shillings per week. This apart, he regularly volunteered to do the farming chores, and was equally as proficient working the land. The situation seemed ideal for all parties concerned. Wood was no problem and the Smiths had in fact taken to him. He appeared to respect his employers, and he quickly settled into the community.

However, as time progressed, James Wood's standard and quantity of work dropped significantly. There was no apparent outside problem which would account for this and he still managed to earn sufficient to pay his

The parish of Bromfield – quiet and remote – hardly changed since the terrible events of January 1808.

board but had little else on top. Integration into the community had seen him make several liaisons with unattached local women, so perhaps the late nights and extra financial burdens such relationships can create were too much for him to maintain. Whatever the reason, he kept his own counsel.

As time progressed, Wood was utilised as a traveller-journeyman, selling the woven products at market and considered trustworthy enough to return with all monies received and accounted for. It seems likely that Thomas Smith offered him this opportunity in the hope that it would revive his enthusiasm for his work, and of course keep him at Longburn in their employment. As the travelling workload was shared, each man would either work the farm or work the markets.

18

On the morning of 19th January 1808, Thomas Smith was up early, loading his cart for Wigton market. It was a relatively short journey, but Wigton was then renowned for being a difficult selling point. Travellers would look for the best bargains and would often delay purchases until late evening when the traders were more desperate to sell. Thomas Smith was a little more fortunate than most; being fairly local, the residents of Wigton would visit his cart as regular clients. It was bitterly cold that day and Smith, heavily wrapped in clothing, stood by the back of his cart selling his goods. The cold blast of winter was always a good time for him, as people clamoured for those woven wraps to provide extra warmth.

By that evening, he had very little left to sell. It had been a good day, although the freezing cold wind had now been worsened by driving rain which stung his face as he made the journey home. Thomas was looking forward to getting home, knowing that James would have tended to the farm, leaving nothing to be done till morning. Margaret and Jane were responsible for looking after the cattle, housing them in the barn and cleaning out the yard. It was a chore which offered variety from the often laborious weaving tasks.

As he drove the cart into the yard of his farm, he was somewhat bewildered to see the cattle still out, huddled together in the driving rain. He quickly alighted, housed and fed his horse and removed what was left of his goods from the rear of the cart, taking them into the house. 'Margaret? Jane? Where are you? The cattle are still out, why have you not brought them in?'

When Thomas walked into the kitchen, seated at the large wooden table was his sister-in-law, Jane Pattinson. The woman was slumped forward, her head resting on her arms on the table before her. Smith shook her but got no response. 'Jane, wake up. What has occurred here?'

19

Raising her head, he saw that it was covered in blood, and that she was clearly in an unconscious state. He searched the house for Margaret and James, but there was no sign of them.

Searching his mind for an explanation, he came to the conclusion that Jane had fallen and hurt herself. Margaret and James had probably gone in search of someone to treat her injuries. In view of this he felt there was little else for him to do, so he braved the winter's night to bring in the cattle. It was a simple task, the cattle were ready to come and within the space of three or four minutes had been housed in the barn and provided with an amount of feed.

Smith then checked everything else on the farm to ensure that he would not have to venture out again. Satisfied that everything was as it should be, he returned to the farmhouse.

He lit a candle and went over to Jane, who had now regained some form of consciousness and was making gurgling noises. 'Are you all right?' he asked. Again he tried to sit her up but this time, assisted by the light of the candle, he saw that this was far more serious than he had first thought. Jane had clearly been attacked by someone wielding a sharp weapon. Some of the fingers of her left hand were all but severed and were hanging limply by a piece of skin. Her head displayed a severe wound right across the forehead as though sliced by the blade of a knife, and her throat was cut. Within seconds she collapsed forward, her head striking the table with a sickening thump. She felt no further pain, she was dead.

Thomas Smith was horrified. Who could have done such a thing? His immediate concern was for Margaret. Where could she be? He carried out another frantic, but more thorough, search of the house, calling out his wife's name, but to no avail. No reply was received and no trace of his wife could be found. He visited James Wood's

20

quarters, but again there was no sign of him anywhere.

It is difficult to know what goes through a man's mind at such times, but clearly Thomas Smith was in a panic-stricken state. In 1808 there was no form of instant communication available to him, no immediate solution to aid him in his search for answers.

Satisfying himself that Margaret was not in the house, he decided to carry out a search of the farm outhouses and barns. He did not have to go too far before his worst fears became reality. In one of the barns lay the body of Margaret Smith. She too had suffered horrific head injuries, which Smith later described, 'her head was as soft as a turnip, her skull was very much cracked.'

With no further thought in his mind, he fled from the barn and ran as fast as his legs would carry him to a neighbouring farm, screaming out 'Murder! Murder!' as he did so. Within the hour, the farm was swarming with people, most of the parish turning out to view the carnage.

There was no doubt, James Wood was nominated as being prime suspect. At this time, the police force as we know it did not yet exist in anything but a basic form; there were still watchmen guarding the routes through Workington, Maryport and Carlisle up to Border country. These watchmen were not a professional body of men, but were little better than the criminals they pursued, paid a pittance to protect the inhabitants of the various towns and parishes which they had been delegated to patrol. Constables did exist, one per parish, but were basically forced 'volunteers' carrying out the role without payment, secondary to their own work. Many were labourers, or those without influence who found the role forced upon them. Some, believe it or not, were very good at what they did. The local Longburn constable detailed villagers to search outhouses and buildings in the parish. Any sightings of Wood were to be reported immediately, indeed he was to be detained on suspicion of murder.

Smith sat in the empty farmhouse, trying to find a reasonable explanation for the atrocity, of which, of course there was none. The motive had clearly been theft, for a sealed box normally kept in the parlour had been opened. His wife kept the key on her person. The contents of the box – a 20 shilling note and a crown piece, the property of Jane; half-a-crown, the property of his wife; and three shillings belonging to him – were missing. As too was another half-crown which belonged to his wife and was of sentimental value; it was of the coinage of William and Mary and had been stamped 'MP 1802', his wife's initials. Also missing was Thomas Smith's pocket watch.

Messengers were despatched throughout the Border country and Lancashire, providing a description of the now absent James Wood, as the whole of Cumberland was horrified by the news of such a maniac being on the loose. Within 24 hours, information was received as to his whereabouts.

Wood had headed north to Scotland, where an alert traveller, hearing of the crime and aware of the description of the wanted man, encountered him in the Tolbooth public house in Annan. The local magistrate, a Mr Scott, assisted by Robert Elliot the local constable, went to the Tolbooth and at once identified their quarry. The magistrate confronted Wood, 'Do you have a watch of any kind which you have purchased recently?' The reply was a simple 'No'.

Detained in a local holding-house, Wood was searched and in the lining of his hat was found a pocket watch! A further search uncovered a shilling, a watch chain, some halfpence and a knife. Concealed with the pocket watch was a half-crown piece bearing the marking 'MP 1802', a crown piece, four half-crowns and 30 shillings. The evidence was overwhelming. All the items found during the search of his clothing were then sealed in a paper envelope before him, to be used as incriminating evidence at the trial.

James Wood was clearly repentant of his actions, and made a full confession to the crime when brought before Justices of the Peace, Sir William Douglas, Mr Greenwood, Mr Hodgson and Mr Forest. He was subsequently tried and found guilty of the double murder and was executed at Carlisle on 25th August 1808.

3

THE NETHERBY BURGLARS

**THE MURDER OF PC JOSEPH BYRNES AT PLUMPTON,
OCTOBER 1885**

Ask any interested resident of Cumbria of the most infamous murder case in the history of the county and you will probably get the same answer – Rudge, Martin and Baker. Unfortunately, it is also one of the most misrepresented cases of all time, with so many myths and legends deriving from it as to confuse the best of researchers.

The story begins over 300 miles from Cumbria, in Essex, when on the night of Tuesday, 20th January 1885 Inspector Simmons was shot and fatally wounded on a country road between Hornchurch and Upminster. The policeman had spotted three suspicious individuals lurking in the bushes close to a country home. As he and a constable approached the group, one of the men turned upon the officer and shot him. He later died, on 28th January 1885, as a result of the injuries sustained. Before the shooting started he had told his colleague that he recognised two of the group as local criminals. One of them, a man known as David Dredge, was arrested in Stepney, London, by Detective Sergeant Rolfe of the Metropolitan Police and taken to Romford for questioning. He confessed to being part of the trio, further informing the authorities that the other two men they wanted were James Lee and John White, alias John Martin.

Lee was arrested and tried alongside Dredge; Lee was found guilty and executed, Dredge acquitted. Despite this, the Essex force were still desperate to trace the third member of the gang, the one whom they believed to be the most dangerous, John Martin. The wait was to be a long one. Detective Sergeant Rolfe, who detained Dredge, also knew Martin. One afternoon whilst walking in Commercial Road, Whitechapel, he came across the wanted man and approached him. Martin turned on the officer, produced a pistol from his coat pocket and pointed it between the policeman's eyes. 'If you do not want your brains blown out, you will bugger off now, understand?' Rolfe had little alternative but to let his man go.

During the months which followed, various country houses were successfully burgled and it was believed that the same gang was responsible. Eleven police forces were involved in the investigation as the crimes spread throughout the country.

By October 1885 the burglaries had reached the north west of England, with Liverpool and Manchester suffering greatly. In Leek, Staffordshire, an officer had spotted three men in some woodland close to a large country house. He approached the group which split in two directions, the constable giving chase after his single quarry (the other two ran off in the opposite direction). As he closed upon the fleeing man, the officer received the shock of his life, as suddenly the man stopped in his tracks, turned to face the oncoming policeman and calmly fired two shots at him. The constable took both shots full on and collapsed to the ground, wounded, but thankfully not fatally.

A description of the man was circulated and he was identified as Anthony Benjamin Rudge, alias William

Fennell or William Walsh, a 45 year old dog trainer from London's East End and a known associate of John Martin! Rudge had previous convictions for housebreaking offences and had only recently been released from prison.

Once again the gang escaped detection and apparently went to ground, that is until Tuesday, 9th October 1885 when they re-emerged at Newton Hall, Stocksfield on Tyne. Once again a daring burglary took place, where the gang raided an upstairs bedroom whilst the family entertained below. This time they were almost caught in the act, and only just managed to escape. Three days later they carried out a further raid at the home of a Mrs Davidson in Benwell, getting away with goods to the value of £30.

Next came Scotland, and on the morning of Saturday, 17th October the gang burgled a secluded railway station aptly titled Crookston, near Glasgow. A safe was removed and jemmied open with £300 being stolen.

Still not satisfied, the gang made their way to Cardonald railway station that same morning, where a similar crime took place, only this time as the gang chiselled away at the safe in a nearby field, the banging and clanging attracted the attention of two constables on patrol. The Lanarkshire bobbies were quick to give chase, but again the gang split, two heading one way and one man the other. Automatically the officers parted company. The constable pursuing the pair suddenly found himself charging down on the two men, both of whom had stopped and were turning to face him. One of the men held a firearm and pointed it directly towards the oncoming officer.

Three loud cracks shattered the peaceful morning as the policeman fell to the ground, and sensibly feigned death. All three shots had in fact missed their target. The men escaped. The other officer managed to secure his

Netherby Hall today.

quarry, who later identified the two escapers as John Martin and Anthony Benjamin Rudge.

Thus we arrive in Cumberland on the night of Wednesday, 28th October 1885. Netherby Hall was the historic seat of the Graham family, situated two miles from Longtown close to the Scottish border. At around 8 pm a housemaid went upstairs to Lady Hermione Graham's bedroom and, curiously, found the door locked from the inside. Unable to gain access, she told the housekeeper. A valet was sent to the rear of the premises and found a ladder, supported upon a garden seat, had been propped up against the window to the bedroom. The valet, Joseph Plenderleath, climbed the ladder and entered Lady Hermione's bedroom through the insecure window. The room was empty and he at once unlocked the bedroom door.

27

Netherby Hall in 1890.

Lady Hermione Graham found that her jewellery box had been forced open, and a small pair of diamond ear drops, three diamond stars, and other jewellery to the value of £1,000 was missing. The police at Longtown were informed and by use of telegraph the Carlisle police were notified, as it was believed that the burglars would head south to the city.

At about 10 pm that same evening, Sergeant Roche and Constable Handley were dispatched from Carlisle towards Kingstown on its northern border. The pair had been told to alert the Kingstown officer, Constable Jacob Johnstone. This was quickly achieved and Handley was instructed by the sergeant to make his way back into Carlisle and go to the Citadel railway station to maintain observations there. Meanwhile, Roche and Johnstone remained at Kingstown. Very soon the officers were approached by four strangers coming from the Longtown direction. Roche asked where they had been. 'What business is that of yours?' came the reply. The sergeant explained to the group that a burglary had taken place at Netherby Hall and that he wished to search them in order to ascertain their innocence.

Upon this, one of the men produced a 'jemmy-type implement' and struck Roche over the head, while within seconds two other members of the group produced revolvers and shot him.

Fortunately, both shots struck his arm and were not fatal. Roche collapsed to the floor as the group set about kicking and battering him. PC Johnstone attempted to prevent the attack but was himself struck several heavy blows. The four men then ran off towards Carlisle.

The two injured officers refused to give up and at once gave chase, with Johnstone making ground on the group. As had happened elsewhere, one of the group stopped and turned upon Johnstone and a single shot was fired, sufficient to fell the constable as the bullet entered his right breast.

Meanwhile, the gunfire had been heard by Constable Handley who was only a few hundred yards away from the incident. He at once recruited the assistance of two local men and began to make his way back towards Kingstown. The four desperadoes were confronted by Handley and his two volunteers. Again, revolvers were produced as the group told Handley and his partners to clear off. Handley had no alternative but to do as he was told.

The injured officers at Kingstown were given urgent medical attention; PC Johnstone's condition was grave, although he was to eventually make a remarkable recovery.

It was approximately three hours later when the men were again sighted. Attempts to cordon off all the main access routes into Carlisle had failed, as the men managed to cross the north/south divide of the river Eden via a railway line. At around 2.15 am a railway employee, John Strong, saw three men (not four as previously encountered by the police at Kingstown) walking along the North British railway line which took them past Carlisle. PC Christopher Fortune of the Carlisle City force was informed of the trio's presence on the track and so went after them.

Within a short time he came upon them and asked what they were up to. Without reply they attacked the lone officer, beating him into an unconscious state before leaving him draped over the railway line in a manner which meant certain decapitation by any train which should use the line. It was a sickening act, but displays how ruthless this gang was. Thankfully, one of the trio had enough mercy to return to Fortune's prostrate body, remove it from the line and roll it down a bank. Fortune lay there for a time, before coming to his senses and managing to crawl back to the signal box, where he raised the alarm. A medical examination later revealed 18 individual wounds to his skull; he was never again fit enough to return to duty.

Railway staff along the route to Lancaster were alerted to the possible presence of the dangerous group and descriptions were forwarded to individual station-masters.

It was to be 17 hours before the men resurfaced, by which time the burglary and its aftermath were common knowledge all over the north of England. Indeed, her Majesty Queen Victoria sent a message to the injured officers stating that her thoughts were with them. The Queen further asked to be updated accordingly of their condition and how the investigation was progressing.

The trio were next sighted at Calthwaite, six or seven miles south of Carlisle, where they asked the stationmaster what time trains south were expected. It was now shortly after 7 pm. The men were informed of the train times and duly walked away from the station in the direction of Plumpton, some two to three miles further south.

The local constable at Plumpton, PC Joseph Byrnes, received this information at around 8.20 pm when he called at Calthwaite station on his rounds. He at once returned to Plumpton. The gang had by now arrived in the village, where two of them entered the Pack Horse Inn and purchased four glasses of beer, some bread and some cheese. They remained in the pub for just five minutes.

At approximately 8.40 pm, the sharp crack of a gunshot shattered the peace of Plumpton. Nobody knew what it was, and although several people noted the time and looked out of their windows, nobody physically sought out the source.

The field where Byrnes' body was found.

Christopher Gaddes – railway guard.

At 10 pm a man leaving the Pack Horse Inn and walking back into the village heard strange groaning sounds coming from behind a stone wall in a nearby field. Initially he thought the sounds were those of distressed cattle, but closer inspection revealed them to be human. They were the desperate cries of PC Byrnes who lay dying in the field, having been shot and dumped there by the gang. PC Joseph Byrnes passed away at a quarter to one the following morning. Blood found on the road some yards from the wall identified the precise location where Byrnes fell wounded.

News of the incident spread quickly through the close knit communities of Cumberland and North Lancashire; one of the most efficient methods was by word of mouth via railway staff, which in this case proved to be an extremely worthwhile exercise.

A few hours after the attack, Christopher Gaddes, a railway guard, saw three men climb on board one of the wagons of his train. It was dark, but he refused to panic. Gaddes told the engine driver not to make the scheduled stop at Shap, but to continue to Tebay. Dramatically, as the train slowed down to pass through Shap station, Gaddes managed to hurl a note out to a colleague on the platform, explaining that he thought the men wanted for the woundings in Carlisle were on board the train and asking for support to be present for their arrival at Tebay.

Several railway employees were waiting at Tebay; Gaddes' message had been successfully passed. The train stopped and Gaddes and his colleagues clambered over the wagons, which were covered by a tarpaulin sheet. Eventually he trod on someone hiding beneath the sheet. Suddenly the three men appeared, leapt out of the wagon and ran off. Characteristically, two went towards Shap while the other ran towards Lancaster. The sole escaper made very little headway as he was knocked flat by foreman porter George Beattie, using his brick stick to

Left to right: Rudge, Martin, Baker.

excellent purpose. The stunned man was then tied up by engine driver William Parker, and a revolver recovered from his coat pocket.

Another of the wanted men tried to clamber over the buttress of a bridge which crossed the river Lune. Pursued, he attempted to remove a revolver from his coat pocket but was quickly cracked over the head with a jack bar. The revolver was recovered and the man detained and tied up. The third man managed to slip away into the darkness, but was sighted at various points along the railway route to Lancaster.

It was at Lancaster that he was finally detained, by yet another railway employee, on the south-bound platform. His coat was pulled from his shoulders down to his elbows, thus restricting arm movement until a rope was found to properly secure him.

The three men were conveyed to Carlisle where they were detained awaiting trial for the murder of PC Byrnes and the burglary at Netherby Hall.

The three men were identified as James Baker, Anthony Benjamin Rudge and John Martin. All three were tried at Carlisle Assizes, during which Rudge admitted firing the fatal shot which killed Byrnes. Despite this

H.M. Theatre, Carlisle
Phone 41

6-40 —— TWICE NIGHTLY —— 8-50

MATINEE, SATURDAY AT 2-30 P.M.

Week commencing Monday, October 17th. ... Important production of Cumberland's Own Great Crime Story:

RUDGE, MARTIN AND BAKER

(A Play in 12 Scenes by Eva Elwes and A. C. Astor)

Being an authentic re-construction of the crimes, arrest, trial and execution of these famous criminals. An Epic Story of Cumberland's Bravery and Loyalty to Duty.

All characters and scenes in the various episodes are faithful representations of the original. . . . The Trial for Murder at the Carlisle Assize Court, is an exact reproduction, word for word, of the original Trial. A unique opportunity for you to see how a murder trial is conducted.

The First Time on any Stage an actual Murder Trial has been presented.

A CUMBERLAND PLAY PRESENTED IN CUMBERLAND'S OWN COUNTY THEATRE

AN EVENT IN THE THEATRICAL HISTORY OF THE NORTH !

CAST OF 48 ARTISTES

The Professional Artistes who play the majority of the parts are augmented by well-known local and other amateurs.

The principle scenes include—The County Police Office ; Plumpton Railway Station ; Pack Horse Inn ; Plumpton Wall ; Tebay Goods Yard ; Lancaster Railway Station ; The Carlisle Assize Court ; The Old Goal Tap ; Carlisle Goal.

A BRIEF HISTORY OF THE CRIMES OF RUDGE, MARTIN AND BAKER.

The history begins with an audacious robbery of jewellery from Netherby Hall, on October 28th, 1885, but being disturbed, the burglars made their way across country in the direction of Carlisle. Three hours later, Sergeant Roche and P.C. Johnstone met them near Kingstown. A struggle ensued in which both officers were shot, and seriously wounded. The men pursued their way to Carlisle, when P.C. Fortune of the City police, observed them on the Canal line. Near Iredale's brewery they turned upon him, beat him savagely about the head and left him insensible, and got away. On the Thursday night, they were encountered near Plumpton, by P.C. Byrnes. They fired at him with fatal effect, and threw his body over a wall, and proceeded on to Penrith. About nine o'clock the same night, at Penrith high goods yard, the brakesman of a luggage train going south saw three men get into a waggon. Surmising that they were the men wanted, the brakesman in passing Shap, threw out a written message upon the platform, urging the stationmaster to telegraph to Tebay to get ready. This evidently was not seen. On reaching Shap summit, the Liverpool night goods train was standing, and the brakesman threw a similar message on to the engine of this train, the driver of which wired to Tebay. The stationmaster at Tebay acted accordingly. Two of the men were seized, but the other escaped up the line, and was eventually arrested at Lancaster. This man (John Baker) was brought to Carlisle by train, in the charge of Supt. Semphill of Carlisle, and Supt. Russell of Brampton. When they emerged from the carriage the scene was uproarious. The crowd could not be controlled, and several attempts were made to lynch the prisoner. The trial at the Carlisle courts resulted in the three prisoners being found guilty, and sentenced to death.

At eight o'clock on the morning of February 8th, 1886, Rudge, Martin and Baker were executed in Carlisle gaol, by the executioner Berry.

The greatest care has been exercised in making this play—many old records have been searched—many relatives and friends of the various characters in the play have helped to make every detail correct, and patrons may regard the production as being historically perfect.

THE PLAY PRODUCED BY PHILLIP STAINTON. THE WHOLE PRODUCTION UNDER THE DIRECTION OF ARTHUR C. CROSBY.

Free List entirely suspended. **Booking Plans now open**

MATINEE, SATURDAY AT 2-30 P.M.

W. Johnston, "Gazette" Printing Office, Globe Lane, Carlisle.

'An event in the theatrical history of the north'.

confession, a clear attempt to exonerate his partners in crime, the three men were found guilty and sentenced to death, their execution taking place on 8th February 1886.

A memorial stone was erected at the site where PC Byrnes was killed in Plumpton. It reads:

'HERE CONSTABLE JOSEPH BYRNES FELL ON
THE NIGHT OF OCTOBER 26 1885, SHOT BY
THE THREE NETHERBY BURGLARS WHOM HE
SINGLE HANDEDLY ENDEAVOURED TO ARREST.'

Some of the stolen property was recovered from the river Lune where it had been dumped by the miscreants during the pursuit, and it was safely returned to the Graham family. However, a solid gold butterfly ring did not turn up until the early 1990s. Inside it bore a strange inscription: 'THIS RING COST FOUR MEN THEIR LIVES, NETHERBY BURGLARS 1886.' It has never been ascertained who had the ring over this period of time. It turned up at Sotheby's in London and was handed back to Sir Charles Graham, whose property it remains.

The myth of the 'fourth man' has grown out of all proportion ever since the crimes took place. Clearly this man left the group before they were seen on the railway line in Carlisle. Much has been made of this man's presence, and why he was with the gang, and why he was never brought to justice.

The police actually arrested the fourth man shortly after the other three were captured. He was a well known criminal, another James Baker, alias James Smith, alias James Johnston. The Metropolitan Police knew him as 'One-armed Jemmy' because of an iron crook he wore on his left arm to replace a hand lost in a work accident. It was probably this which struck Sergeant Roche over the head at Kingstown.

Police intelligence indicates that Baker was a known associate of Rudge, Martin and Baker, and that he had a record for violence and housebreaking. He was also a

The memorial stone to PC Byrnes.

good 'fence' able to dispose of all types of stolen property, no matter how valuable.

One-armed Jemmy was arrested in Regent Street, London by a PC Westwood, as his description had been circulated as being wanted in connection with the crimes in Cumberland. He was at once conveyed to Carlisle and held at Earl Street lock-up. Placed before local magistrates on Thursday, 24th December 1885, he was remanded in custody.

He admitted to being in Longtown at the time of the incident, but denied having been involved in the offence, claiming he was there for a coursing event. Several persons who caught a glimpse of the desperadoes were called in to positively identify Baker as the fourth man, but none were able to do so! Thus with no positive identification, Baker (the fourth man) walked free.

Over the years theories as to the identity of the 'fourth man' have been received from all over the world, creating a myth almost as mysterious as that of Jack the Ripper. Mysteries, however, are in fact of our own making, and the 'mystery' of the fourth man is no more. It never really existed, except in the minds of eager journalists keen to spin the story out.

4

MURDER ON THE HIGH ROAD

THE MURDER OF ISABELLA STEELE NEAR NEWBY, SEPTEMBER 1887

There is nothing as emotive as the murder of a child, no matter what century, no matter what circumstances. Even over 100 years after the event, the story of little Isabella Steele can still fill the reader with horror.

William Hunter was born in Glasgow, but moved to Salford on the outskirts of Manchester with his family when only a young child. Hunter knew nothing of his brief time in Glasgow, but as he grew up he would talk of one day returning to the city. In 1876 he married a local girl and the following year a child was born of the relationship.

For reasons known only to himself, William Hunter disliked the responsibility of fatherhood and duly took off, literally disappearing for seven years. His wife could do little about it; all the usual enquiries were made, but no one knew what had happened to Hunter.

Then one day in 1884 he returned and expected to resume his marriage where he had left it seven years previously. Incredibly, his wife accepted him back and the family lived together in Salford quite contentedly for a further twelve months.

Hunter was trained as a blacksmith's striker and managed to gain employment which provided for all the needs of his family. There were one or two teething problems in the relationship, but all in all things seemed to be working out well, although he would never discuss the missing seven years. Once a week he would go out drinking, returning home late and generally the worse for wear. On one occasion he caused trouble in a Salford street. The police arrived and asked him to move on but Hunter was in no mood to do as he was told and duly thumped the officer as hard as he could. It took three further officers to restrain him and he was later charged with assault.

When a second child was born it once again seemed too much for Hunter to accept. His moods changed; he was now becoming violent and would think nothing of giving his wife a good hiding. Then he walked out on his wife and children for a second time, and this time he was never to return.

Hunter took to tramping around the north of England. Here he had no responsibilities and could do as he wished whenever he wished. Whilst in Scotland in early August 1887 he met with a lady of the road, a 32 year old by the name of Mary Steele, who had an illegitimate daughter aged three and a half years named Isabella. Hunter swept the woman off her feet; both were in desperate need of company and they were attracted to one another. The pair decided that they should travel together as common law man and wife.

Later that month Hunter and his new companions visited Carlisle, where they stayed for a week at Mrs Green's common lodging house in Peascod Lane in the city. During this spell Mr and Mrs Green grew concerned over the state of young Isabella. Certain bruises and marks on the child's body indicated some form of abuse but when the Greens approached the child's mother, she refused to discuss the matter any further, denying any maltreatment. Isabella could be heard crying, painfully sobbing late at night and at all hours of the morning.

Every so often her cries would be cut short by a burst of verbal abuse from William Hunter.

A week later the couple left the Greens and continued on their travels. Mr Green was to later say that he felt Mary to be frightened of Hunter, but not to the extent that she was too scared to speak her mind. Both adults liked a drink, and both consumed their fair share, taking the young child into pubs with them.

On the night of Wednesday, 7th September 1887 they arrived in Wigton and obtained lodgings in the town. The trio remained there overnight before setting off at about 9.30 the following morning. They told the lodging-house keeper that it was their intention to head for Carlisle, then perhaps on to Scotland, and Glasgow where Hunter hailed from.

Mary Steele was herself a Scottish girl, born in Old Cumnock, Ayrshire. She would talk of Scotland and impress Hunter with her tales of its picturesque beauty. Never did it cross his mind to ask why, if it was so quaint, so idyllic, she was in England.

Mary Steele was no angel, she too had the odd conviction for theft, and had slept around to earn her keep before latching onto William Hunter. The reality of it all was that they were deceiving each other. For Hunter, Steele was easy sex and a partner on his travels. He despised young Isabella and whenever possible tried to avoid contact with her. Mary used Hunter as a minder, who would look after her interests, provide a roof over her head, scrounge and steal for her. The pair of them were little more than malicious vagrants.

Along the route to Carlisle from Wigton, which was then known as the High Road, the young child began to cry. She was tired and hungry and could hardly walk. Her little feet were aching and bruised from the constant smacks with a stick which Hunter would dish out whenever she cried. It was around 5 pm on the afternoon

41

of the 8th September and the trio had just passed Newby
when Isabella collapsed, exhausted.

Any normal man would have stopped to care for the
child's needs, even to pick her up and carry her for a
while. Not William Hunter, he simply hit her over the
head with a heavy stick and continued to strike her until
she got up and again began to walk. Isabella was still
crying.

Mary sat down to rest and told Hunter to do the same,
'Perhaps Bella will calm down if we rest a short while.'
'I'll be damned if she will hold us up, woman, we must
get on our way. It's not far to Carlisle, come on, get up.'
With this he kicked the resting child firmly in the back.
There was a sickening crunch as his boot connected and
Isabella fell backwards onto the grass. Her tears had
stopped, she would feel no further pain; the mighty blow
of Hunter's leather boot upon her frail little back was
sufficient to render a fatal blow which killed her outright.

It was only when Hunter looked down at the child's
expressionless face that he knew he had caused her
serious harm. Quickly he bent down and picked her up.
'Bella, Bella, wake up, my God help me, Bella, God bless
you!' Mary Steele still did not realise that her daughter
was dead and told Hunter to stop his antics and to put
Isabella down. The terrified man ran for some water and
returned a few moments later, splashing it on Isabella's
face and trying to force it down her throat in a vain
attempt to get her to swallow. It was too late for any of
that, Hunter had killed the child.

In blind panic more than anything else, Hunter pushed
Mary Steele away, wrapped the child in a shawl and
carried her in his arms across a field. He was devastated;
not, one suspects, remorseful, but more frightened as to
the consequences of his actions. He then placed the child
on the ground beneath a hedgerow on the far side of the
field. Agitated, he walked away from the body down the

field, and took from his pocket a knife and attempted to slit his own throat.

Mary Steele, still not aware of what had happened, followed him and told him to get up. It suddenly dawned on her that Hunter had two gaping gashes in his neck from which a large amount of blood was oozing. Frantic, she fled across the field and onto the road, running as fast as she could towards Carlisle. After a short distance she met a farmer in his cart. Mr Aitchison asked her what the problem was and was told in no uncertain terms that it was a matter of life and death.

The farmer drove into Carlisle and met with Constable Arthur Baker of the Carlisle City Police in Wigton Road. Baker got into the trap and returned to the spot the woman had identified. This was approximately 150 yards away from Morton Cottage, the field being on the right-hand side of the road.

Constable Baker ran across the field and saw a woman standing over a bundle on the ground, which he realised was the dead body of a young child. 'The man with whom I am travelling has killed this child,' she told the officer. 'Where is that man now?' asked Baker. Mary Steele pointed further down the field, where Baker saw the body of a man laid upon the ground.

The man was face down with both his arms tucked beneath his body. Baker rolled him over and saw that in one hand he clasped a knife, the blade of which was saturated in blood. The man was still breathing and at once PC Baker tied the man's neckerchief tight around his neck in an attempt to stem the flow of blood from the two wounds in the front of his throat, next to the windpipe. A fellow police officer, Constable Kirkpatrick, arrived at the scene having heard of the incident via tittle tattle spreading from the original message overheard being passed to PC Baker. The two officers carried the wounded man on a gate back to the road. A young lad by the name of McGloan collected the body of the child and carried that to the roadside where it was at once conveyed to Mr Thursby's public house at Raffles. Hunter was taken to the Cumberland Infirmary for treatment to his injuries.

Mary Steele was taken to Earl Street lock-up where she was to be detained for a brief time, at least until after the inquest. The police were concerned that they had only her story to go by. If she had lied then, as a vagrant, she could make her escape and probably never be seen again. Thus to prevent any problems it was decided that her detention was in the best interests of all concerned.

On the evening of the crime, Inspector Roche (himself something of a local hero – see The Netherby Burglars) recorded a statement of events from Mary Steele. This read: 'I am 32 years of age, and am a single woman belonging to Old Cumnock, Ayrshire. I had an illegitimate child named Isabella Steele; she was three years old past. I took up with William Hunter, and lived with him as his wife. We have been tramping the country since. On Wednesday night we were at Wigton. We stopped at a lodging-house there. We left Wigton between nine and ten this morning. My little girl was bad-tempered on the road. William Hunter beat her. When we came to near Carlisle we sat down on the road. Hunter gave my little girl a kick on the back. He then lifted her up and said "Bella, God bless you." He ran and got some water and put it on the little girl. He lifted her off the road, and wrapped a plaid about her, and carried her off into a field nearby. The little girl was then dead. I saw him go into the field. He went down-field about 150 yards. He laid the little girl down on the ground, and cried to me, "Come, I want you." He went further down the field, and when I went to see what he was doing I saw he had cut his throat with a knife. I screamed for help, and a woman came to me. I had nothing to do with the murder of my

44

child. William Hunter is the man who murdered my child.'

At the subsequent inquest into the child's death held on 10th September, several witnesses were called to give evidence. It transpired that a number of people had witnessed Hunter either punch, kick or strike the child with some weapon over a period of time. Doctor Lediard told how he found bruises on just about every part of the girl's body imaginable. There was some suggestion that Hunter had carried out minor sexual assaults upon the child, though this was never substantiated in court.

A verdict of wilful murder was returned, and Hunter, who until that point had lain in Cumberland Infirmary, was duly declared fit and well enough to be transferred to the county gaol. In his defence all that Hunter would say was that Isabella was a bad child. On the day in question he had kicked her legs from beneath her, causing her to fall over and crack her head against a milestone.

Hunter was ultimately found guilty of wilful murder and sentenced to death. An appeal was lodged with the Home Secretary on various grounds. The main supporting evidence for this appeal was that Hunter was not a man of bad character, the incident involving Isabella had been an unfortunate accident. It was even claimed that Hunter was more of a parent to the child than her natural mother, Mary Steele.

The appeal was turned down, no evidence was found to support these claims and when one considers the testimonies of other witnesses, all of whom claimed to have seen Hunter beating the child, then there can be no doubting that this was a correct verdict.

Hunter was sent to the gallows on 14th November 1887. The executioner, James Berry, was informal in his dealings with the condemned man, speaking with him as though they were best of friends. At eight o'clock that morning William Hunter danced his way to death, dropping six feet into Berry's pit.

Outside the prison only a few hundred people had gathered, many of them women and children. There were no cheers and no remorse, just silence as the black flag was hoisted. Mary Steele was of course an innocent party in these circumstances, although it has to be said that she hardly showed the devotion one would expect of a natural mother to her child. There can be no forgiving William Hunter for his crime.

5

THE BREAKFAST KILLER

THE MURDER OF MARION CROSSMAN AT HAVERIGG, JANUARY 1892

The most puzzling of all criminals has to be the outwardly normal individual whose momentarily irrational behaviour causes them to kill for what can be the most ridiculous of reasons. Such a crime took place in Haverigg, near Millom in 1892.

Haverigg is situated on a peninsula which faces out into the Irish Sea. It is a somewhat remote area, where the townsfolk know each other and are to a certain extent aware of each other's movements and routines. At one time the majority of its inhabitants were occupied at the shipyards in the nearby Furness region.

Joseph Wilson came to Haverigg in April 1891 when he gained employment at a local quarry. He came from Kendal, where his father, William, was a hawker, and he was one of three sons. The Wilson family had had more than their fair share of problems over the years. Prior to Joseph's birth, his mother, Margaret, lost her sanity and suffered greatly from fits. Her condition never improved and whenever William left the house he was forced to lock Margaret in a room until he returned, so concerned was he that she would cause harm to the children. Insanity appeared to run in the family as William also had a cousin who was incarcerated in an asylum.

Joseph Wilson had started work on the railway as a 16 year old, when he was employed as a pointsman in

Barrow where the family had originally lived. However, when sickness and economics forced them to move from the area to Kendal, Joseph resigned from his position and assisted his father in hawking. Now he returned to the area for a new start.

Joseph was a shy young man, illiterate and of a wiry build. He was described at the time as 'under developed' but whether this gauges his mentality or physique, one cannot be certain. What we do know is that he was a hard working young man, keen to please and reasonably well liked by all who knew him.

When he returned to the area he contacted an old friend, Richard Crossman, whom he had known since his previous employment on the railway. Dick was older than he, married for a second time, and had some seven children, two from his previous marriage. Dick's wife, Marion Greaves Crossman, was a friendly woman and she too respected Wilson, having no misgivings about him lodging with them. They all lived at a residence known as The Hill, but moved to number 4, Moor Moss Cottages in September 1891, along with Joseph Wilson.

Joseph was now engaged to one of Dick Crossman's daughters. Everything had been arranged for the wedding and the couple were saving hard to rent a house of their own. A few days before Christmas, both Joe Wilson and Dick Crossman went out to purchase a few items of furniture for the future home. Joseph was obviously liked and accepted as part of the family.

On New Year's Eve 1891 the Crossman household had been invited to number 2, Moor Moss Cottages, the home of James and Mary Ann Johns. Many of the neighbours popped in throughout the evening. Shortly before midnight the Crossmans returned home. The children were about worn out, the excitement of a late night and the end of the Christmas festivities had caught up with them.

48

Joe Wilson himself left the Johns' house a little after midnight, believing that it was only manners to stay and greet the new year with his hosts. There was no over indulgence in alcohol, no over zealous incidents, just good humoured sociable fun. When he returned home, Joe found that the rest of the Crossman household had retired. Silently he crept to his room and went to sleep.

It was around 7 am the following morning, that of New Year's Day, when Marion Crossman awoke and made her way downstairs to carry out her usual chores. Joe Wilson came down about 40 minutes later and sat quietly by the fire playing games with one of the children. Richard Crossman came down shortly after; he had some work to do in Barrow and duly left the house at ten minutes to eight. He was later to recall, 'everything was peaceful that morning, no unpleasantness, just normal.'

A few moments later, Marion Crossman was asked by Wilson, 'Where's my breakfast then?' 'You'll have to wait for that, I am far too busy Joe,' was her reply. 'Too busy, damn you woman, I want my breakfast.' Suddenly Joe flew into a blind rage. Marion was horrified, she had never before witnessed this side of Joe's character. However, being a sensible woman she decided that it would be best to ignore it.

Marion kept herself busy but found an uncomfortable atmosphere in the cottage that morning. Joe seemed to be watching her every movement. Indeed, at one point he grabbed hold of her as though about to force his attentions upon her. Again Marion was in control of the situation, she pushed him away and laughed it off as if it was a practical joke.

Deep down she was very concerned, and at 20 minutes to nine that morning she went next door, to number 3, Moor Moss Cottages, the home of Jane Coles. 'Jane, I am a bit worried about Joe, he seems odd this morning. I think he is going to ravish me.' Jane Coles dismissed her fears and told Marion to sit down. Marion had visited her neighbour on the pretext of having a New Year drink and she had taken a small bottle of rum with her. She poured them both a rum as the women sat and discussed what the future twelve months might have in store for them.

Within a few minutes, Joe Wilson knocked on Jane Coles' front door. The woman answered, 'Hello, Joe. Happy New Year, love.' Joe looked a little groggy, as though he had been drinking. 'Where's Mrs Crossman?' he asked. 'Not here,' said Jane and closed the door. Marion Crossman was terrified, she had hidden away when Joe appeared at the door – curious actions for a woman who had previously implicitly trusted her lodger.

Marion remained with Jane Coles for a good three-quarters of an hour. After that she wanted to go home, but was frightened to do so in case Joe did something out of character. Jane decided to go and find out where Wilson was and left Marion in her home whilst she went in search of him. Joe was in fact back at the Johns' home, drinking beer and talking gibberish about the Crossman family and how he felt they sometimes did not want him there!

Jane Coles heard all of this and decided not to stay, so returned to her own home, but was followed by Joseph Wilson. Marion Crossman secreted herself in the coal house when she saw Wilson enter the house. 'You can come out, I know you are here,' said Wilson. Marion then came out of hiding and smiled placatingly at Wilson, who reciprocated. The trio were soon joined by Mrs Johns, and all consumed further glasses of rum.

Wilson then told Marion Crossman to go back home and to get his breakfast ready. 'You'll have to bloody well wait, I will make it in my own time, not when you demand it,' she snapped back at Joseph. Both Mrs Johns and Marion Crossman then left the house and returned to their own homes. Jane Coles told Joseph Wilson to get out of her house as she no longer wanted him there. 'Your breakfast will be ready, will it not? You have found Mrs Crossman, now clear off home.'

Joe Wilson laughed at Jane and said, 'Some person will have had their breakfast in two hours!' He then left.

At approximately 10.30 that same morning neighbours of the Crossman household heard the report of a gun and the muffled sound of something heavy thudding onto the floor. The noise clearly emanated from number 4, Moor Moss Cottages.

For a while there was silence. Nobody in any of the cottages moved, as though united in some strange act of mimicry. Then, tentatively, heads peered round front doors and looked in the direction of number 4. There was no movement, and nothing unusual, yet what had been heard was definitely abnormal.

Jane Coles ran to the house and peered through the front windows, but all she could see was the dark figure of Joe Wilson standing motionless at the back of the room. Jane pushed open the front door and there saw the body of Marion Crossman. The woman was laying face down in a pool of blood. It was a scene Jane Coles would never forget. As she struggled to take it in, she also noticed blood and brain matter splattered all over two walls of the cottage. Jane Coles was violently sick.

Joseph Wilson stood between the front room and the kitchen, close to the foot of the stairs. 'How could you do this? What have you done?' Jane yelled incoherently. Wilson showed no sign of emotion, and calmly replied to the neighbour, 'The first one to set foot inside this house will be done, now clear off.'

The alarm was raised and Dr Dunne of Millom was called. He took one look at Marion Crossman and declared her dead. The entire right side of her face had been blown away, from the centre parting in her hair down to her throat; death had been instantaneous. Police

Constable George Currie was summoned and arrived at the scene to find the body of Mrs Crossman where it had fallen, her head a short distance from the front door. Jane Coles told the officer that Wilson was the perpetrator of the crime.

PC Currie asked Wilson (who was standing outside the cottage, seemingly enjoying a cigarette) if that was correct, but Wilson made no reply. The policeman knew he had to take any suspect into custody as soon as possible, so Joseph Wilson was arrested. 'You need not be in such a hurry, I am not going to run away. I bloody well did it. I was not sure I had done it so I put another cartridge in the gun to bloody well make sure of it,' said Joe Wilson.

A short time later, Inspector Watson arrived on the scene and assisted Constable Currie in conveying Wilson to Millom police station. Along the way Wilson said, 'I made a bloody good job of it, did I not? First shot, direct hit. I will likely get my neck stretched for this, won't I?'

Richard Crossman returned home shortly after 3 pm on the day of the crime. He was appalled by the news of his wife's death, and would not believe that such a quiet young man as Joe Wilson would, or could, commit such an atrocity.

Wilson was tried at the Carlisle Assizes in January 1892. It was a relatively short trial in view of the fact that Wilson did not deny the crime with which he was charged. His defence counsel attempted to prove that Joseph was in fact without control of his senses and actions at the time of the murder. It was introduced into court that his mother had suffered from mental problems, as too had other close relatives.

The prosecution stressed that Joseph Wilson had always been a perfectly normal and healthy human being. Constable George Currie gave evidence and said, 'If ever I had to identify a murderer, the last person I would suspect would have been Joseph. He has always been courteous, even after his arrest he caused no problems.' The insanity plea clearly diminished at that point in the proceedings.

Joe Wilson was found guilty of murder and sentenced to death. An appeal was lodged on the ground of his alleged insanity, but was refused.

Throughout his time in the condemned cell at Carlisle gaol, Joe Wilson was polite to his keepers. At night he would smoke his blackened clay pipe and sit peacefully reminiscing over the better moments of his life. Every so often he would tell one of the warders how sorry he was that he killed Marion Crossman.

The night before the execution, Wilson slept well and ate one good meal. At 7 am on the morning of 22nd March 1892, he arose and enthusiastically devoured a bowl of porridge. He then dressed in a suit which his family had brought for him, and awaited the arrival of the hangman.

At 7.45 am the prison bell began sounding, as the executioner, James Billington entered the condemned cell and prepared Wilson for the drop. At 8 am it was all over. Joe Wilson had been dispatched with great efficiency.

Outside the gaol, the crowds which filled the greater part of the Viaduct and English Street were silent. Many tears were spilled when the black flag was hoisted as notification that the execution had been carried out. It was rumoured that one woman wept uncontrollably, and whipped many of the assembled throng into a veritable frenzy as she claimed to be a relative of the executed man and was convinced of his insanity.

Joseph Wilson was in fact the last man to hang in Carlisle. Ever since, in the annals of criminal history, he has been known as the 'Breakfast Killer'.

6

DEATH IN WOOLPACK YARD

THE DEATH OF JAMES GILPIN AT KENDAL, MARCH 1904

Kendal is a smart, tidy town located to the south of the Lake District. In 1902 it was described as: 'A most important road centre, and the gateway from the South for the English Lake District. The town stands on the river Kent and has several ancient buildings.' Little could the author of that brief descriptive passage have known, that at that time Kendal also housed a murderer!

Elizabeth Nicholson was not a particularly attractive female. Somewhat sour faced with sharp prominent features, she found male company hard to come by. And although beauty is only skin deep, Elizabeth was in fact a dense and rather dull individual, with a foul mouth and little in the way of intellect.

Life in Westmorland in the early part of the 20th century offered little in the way of employment for such people. Those with no ties but with intelligence or skills moved to one of the larger towns where good work could be found. The exceptions to the rule, and there are many, were those who were born to work on the land, family and relatives of farm people who generally remained loyal to the same employer for many years, generation through generation.

Elizabeth Nicholson, then aged 41, had little going for her. That is, until she met with James Gilpin, a 63 year old

Elizabeth Nicholson.

farmer who worked the land at Kentmere, near Kendal. Gilpin had been a hard-working man for much of his life and had amassed a small fortune, sufficient to keep him happy for the rest of his days. The old man met Elizabeth in 1884 and, in a strange way, the pair were drawn to each other, as James befriended Elizabeth and eventually asked her to move in with him as housekeeper.

It was a strange request. His own wife had died some time earlier and he had two sons living there with him, one of whom was around the same age as Elizabeth. From the start it was clear what the outcome of this so-called 'business only' venture was going to be. From Elizabeth's point of view, she had a roof over her head and access to funds, all for a few sexual favours and a bit of cleaning work.

Immediately after she moved into Gilpin's home, one of the sons packed his bags and left home, never to return and never to speak with his father again. James Gilpin seemed unaffected by this; he had found a new passion.

James Gilpin fathered five children from his relationship with Elizabeth Nicholson, and despite the couple living together for almost 18 years, there were many in the community who frowned upon the liaison. Talk was rife, but it mattered little to Elizabeth. After 18 years she had grown accustomed to it, and generally anticipated secret whispers when she walked by. In response, she would nod and give a friendly but knowing grin. This ensured that she was kept at arms' length by the locals, who referred to her as a 'strange woman'.

As the farm work grew too much for Gilpin, who was by now 81 years old, he sold up and moved into Kendal. If they thought the gossip would cease, they were wrong. The family moved to a cottage in Woolpack Yard, situated to the rear of the Woolpack Hotel in the town. Entrance to the Yard was made via a large archway, allowing access for vehicles, and it opened up into a

Thomas Metcalfe.

reasonably lengthy street with a row of brick cottages running along both sides. It still exists today, and apart from some modernisation, is much the same. There were many in the town who knew of the couple's personal circumstances, and who ensured any rumours were circulated with great efficiency.

In Woolpack Yard, however, all was well. The family got on with many of their near neighbours who appeared to care little about the couple's background. Everything seemed fine, that is until fate played yet another cruel trick in this liaison.

Sometime in December 1903 a new man moved into Woolpack Yard. His name was Thomas Metcalfe; a dark haired man with a rugged hard-working appearance, he had recently been discharged from the army and had returned to Kendal to live with his stepmother, whose cottage was immediately opposite Gilpin's home.

Later that month, both Metcalfe and Nicholson were seen out together, and it was quite clear from their actions that they were on intimate terms. Poor James Gilpin was now more or less bedridden, his legs and back causing him a great deal of pain.

Worse was to come. With Gilpin unable to get downstairs he was now restricted to his bedroom, and was unaware of what was occurring elsewhere within his home. Elizabeth had Thomas Metcalfe move in with her, sleeping downstairs so the old man upstairs would be none the wiser.

Thomas Metcalfe clearly played the dominant role in the partnership. He had a paltry pension from the army, hardly sufficient to keep him in beer. Thus he used Elizabeth not only for sex, but for all the comforts of home, courtesy of James Gilpin. This meant her drawing heavily upon the old man's savings. When the money temporarily ran out, Nicholson would pawn items of Gilpin's clothing which she knew full well he would never again require. Soon, the whole of the town was talking about Elizabeth Nicholson and her relationship with Metcalfe.

In charge of James Gilpin's financial affairs was a fine man by the name of Alderman John Monkhouse, then Mayor of Kendal. Monkhouse was an accountant and had established over the years a friendship with Gilpin, whom he had represented for some time in one form or another. A short time prior to Metcalfe moving into Gilpin's home, Monkhouse, in agreement with the old man, had arranged an allowance of £3 a week for Elizabeth Nicholson, to cover housekeeping tasks.

Monkhouse realised that Nicholson was fraudulently obtaining funds from James Gilpin's account; on more than one occasion she had forged his name. The money was going direct to Metcalfe, who wasted it. With this in mind, John Monkhouse warned Elizabeth Nicholson that he knew about the fraud, and also told Gilpin, who refused to allow him to inform the authorities.

Monkhouse was disgusted by the state of the house, especially Gilpin's bedroom which was little better than a sewer. 'Why aren't you looking after him, woman?' he demanded of Nicholson. 'None of your damned business, now get out and don't come back,' she retorted.

John Monkhouse refused to do as he was asked and returned to Gilpin's room. 'Are you aware that this shameless woman is bringing embarrassment upon you? She is spending all your money, pawning your clothing, and has another man living downstairs.' 'It's not true, James,' Elizabeth replied. 'The man is Thomas Metcalfe, the man who sometimes reads to you.'

James Gilpin was clearly shocked by this news and told Elizabeth to get out of his room. He then told Monkhouse to carefully monitor his finances, adding that Elizabeth refused to help him downstairs, but he would get down somehow so as to keep an eye on things.

On 20th March 1904, Elizabeth Nicholson visited John Monkhouse at his chambers. 'James is dead. He has suffered badly these past few days with sickness. I think there is something under the master's will for me?' Monkhouse was shocked, yet not truly surprised, as the old man had not been well. Elizabeth's actions, however, were not those one would expect from a grieving next of kin.

The accountant searched for James Gilpin's will and informed Nicholson that she was only entitled to the furniture, valued at about £5. There was £100, but that had been left for the children, not for her. Elizabeth was furious. 'I am better than his wife. You have cheated me, that money is mine, it was I who raised the family. What am I to do now?' John Monkhouse told her that whatever she did was her business, but as executor of James's will, he would ensure that it was strictly adhered to.

The following day, John Monkhouse went to pay his last respects to the body of James Gilpin. Whilst there he was confronted by Elizabeth. 'People say I killed him. Why are they being so cruel? They say I poisoned him. He was my husband for God's sake, I would not do such a thing.'

Kendal's mayor told her to ignore such tales, but pointed out that after all, she had been the author of her own problems, especially after her relationship with Metcalfe had been exposed.

The following day he received an anonymous letter which read: 'Sir, I write to tell you that Elizabeth Nicholson bought a quantity of blue arsenic from Hope's chemist, she poisoned the old man with this. It is a fact I tell you sir, the woman murdered her husband for his possessions.'

Elsewhere in the town other factors were now coming into contention. Richard Gilpin believed Elizabeth had murdered his father. 'People have told me of her plans

Richard Gilpin.

Elizabeth Nicholson before her acquittal.

with Metcalfe, they are to marry at Easter.' This supposition was further confirmed when local people told of how Metcalfe had been openly bragging of his impending marriage to Nicholson at Easter, adding that Elizabeth would be coming into a fair bit of money from the old man's death, which would be 'at any time now'. Another local resident, Mrs Bladdes, had been in Hope's when the arsenic was bought by Elizabeth. 'I was there, you know, I saw her buy the poison she killed the old man with,' she eagerly told anyone who was interested.

John Monkhouse, acting the detective, at once visited Hope's chemist's shop and spoke with Richard Hope who confirmed that Nicholson had indeed purchased threepenny worth of blue arsenic. The purpose of the purchase had been, allegedly, to poison rats. This was the one and only time she had bought arsenic from him.

Upon leaving the chemist's shop, which was situated immediately opposite the entrance to Woolpack Yard, John Monkhouse banged on the door of the cottage where Elizabeth Nicholson had lived with James Gilpin. The woman invited him in, and was again free of any obvious signs of grief. 'Now then Elizabeth, explain this letter I have received. It states that you poisoned the old man, and that you bought poison from Hope's!' 'That is correct, I did buy poison. The master told me to, it was for the rats.' Monkhouse told Elizabeth that he had no alternative but to inform the local police.

Later that same afternoon the police arrived at Woolpack Yard with the intention of arresting both Elizabeth Nicholson and Thomas Metcalfe on suspicion of murder. Elizabeth was missing, but Metcalfe was successfully restrained and held in custody at Kendal police station. He vehemently denied having anything to do with the crime, other than viewing the body on the bed shortly after it had been discovered by Elizabeth.

The following morning a post-mortem was held on the

corpse of James Gilpin. A Home Office analyst, Sir Thomas Stevenson, along with the county analyst, Dr Hallon, were present and confirmed the presence of arsenic in the remains. As the news spread that Nicholson was missing, the entire town was in uproar, wondering where she was and who was harbouring her. A popular belief at the time was that she had left Kendal and had taken an amount of arsenic herself, somewhere in the countryside. A local search was made but no trace of the woman could be found.

Then news broke that she had been seen looking out of a window in Mrs Metcalfe's premises, directly opposite her own home. The police called at the house and carried out a search. There in the cellar they found the missing woman, who refused to go quietly, but she was arrested and was dragged screaming from the house and yard, from where she was taken to Kendal police station.

In the subsequent interview and statement recording, Elizabeth gave the following explanation for how the old man had died.

'On Thursday last, Mr Gilpin gave me some money to go and get some blue arsenic to poison rats with. I got threepenny worth at Hope's and at once returned to the house and took it upstairs to let Mr Gilpin see it. He had been in bed since about Christmas, he was not a well man. He told me that I had got the right stuff and to mix it with some fat. I did this and again showed him, he then told me to go and spread it on some bread along with some cheese. I remember we used to do this when we lived on the farm at Kentmere. I was then to put it in all the holes where the rats came from. I did this downstairs and took the rest upstairs, and while I was in the act of putting some down someone came into the house downstairs, so I put it on the chair beside the bed and went downstairs to see who it was. It was Mrs Levens. I went back upstairs to put the rest down for the rats.

Whilst I was doing this the master said, "I've scattered a piece of cheese on the chair, I've picked it up and eaten it by mistake." He said that there was not enough on it to do him any harm.'

Both suspects were then conveyed to Lancaster Castle prison where they were detained pending trial.

The initial inquest was held at Kendal Town Hall on 19th March 1904. The county analyst, Dr Hallon, told the court that he had found sufficient arsenic in the old man's intestines to kill several people, far too much to have been consumed accidentally. He further explained that he had carried out a full examination of the house where the deceased had lived. A thorough inspection of all rat holes revealed not the slightest trace of any poison!

Other neighbours in Woolpack Yard were called to give evidence. Mrs Levens said she had seen Gilpin vomit a black coloured fluid two days before his eventual death. Mrs Nicholson had told her that it was down to the port wine he had consumed earlier in the day. Later, after the old man had died, she had confronted Nicholson and asked her if it was right she had been putting poison down for the rats. Elizabeth admitted this, yet said nothing of James accidentally consuming some poison on a piece of cheese. Even her own children could not recall her mentioning this incident, although one of them, Margaret, recalled Gilpin instructing her to buy some poison.

From all the available evidence there was nothing to implicate Thomas Metcalfe, who was released from custody with all charges against him being dropped. Thus at Appleby Assizes on 28th June 1904, it was Elizabeth Nicholson who stood alone in the dock, charged with the wilful murder of James Gilpin.

Still she refused to admit the crime, despite a great deal of evidence being placed before the court which tended to point to her guilt. Her defence counsel, Mr Shepherd-

Little, worked wonders for her cause. 'This case is based on the flimsiest supposition and suspicion, there is not the slightest positive piece of evidence which indicates my client's proper guilt. Why could someone else in the household not have poisoned the old man, assuming such a lethal dose was deliberately administered in the first place?' This was a clear indication that he suspected Thomas Metcalfe of the crime. It was a marvellous summing up, putting doubt into the minds of all those present, including the jury.

Further questions were raised as to her motive for murder. Financial gain was clearly a favourite. However, Mr Shepherd-Little pointed out, the sum of £100 was not definitely hers, added to which, with him dead she would lose £12 a month housekeeping, £144 a year. Thus, sensibly, it was in her best interests to keep him alive. It was further recalled that she had voluntarily called in a doctor once she had found the body. A picture of Elizabeth Nicholson as being honest yet naive was painted, and left an indelible image printed on the jury members' minds.

The court adjourned while the jury retired to reach its verdict. 'Any question of doubt about the prisoner's guilt must go in the prisoner's favour. If that is the case, then she must be found not guilty, do you understand?' were the last instructions given to the jury.

The wait in the courtroom was unbearable. Elizabeth collapsed in a heap and had to be carried into a rear exercise yard for fresh air. She sobbed and pleaded for mercy, and there was some speculation that she also pleaded for God's forgiveness. Did this mean she was admitting her guilty part in the crime, or was she apologising for leaving the poison in the bedroom? We shall never know.

The jury returned and Elizabeth, flanked by two stern prison warders, stood pale faced, as though resigned to her fate. She looked drawn and desperate, a woman totally devoid of any hope. 'How do you find the prisoner, guilty or not guilty?' 'NOT GUILTY!'

It was an incredible verdict and Elizabeth Nicholson was clearly stunned by the result. She walked from the assizes a free woman, legally innocent of murder.

Perhaps the truth of the matter lay in the fact that Thomas Metcalfe was an arrogant and forceful man. Many believed it was he who had arranged James Gilpin's death, the hold he had over Elizabeth being so strong as to get her to commit the deed. As for the townspeople of Kendal, the majority were pleased that she had been acquitted; just about everyone believed Metcalfe to be the guilty party, thus if one walked free, both should.

We still don't know who really killed James Gilpin. A thorough re-examination of the documentation relating to this case indicates one obvious point – Thomas Metcalfe and Elizabeth Nicholson were extremely fortunate to escape justice. If there was a conspiracy to kill, it was probably Elizabeth who administered the poison, as Metcalfe would have had little opportunity to do so. The motive was probably financial gain, not conceived by Elizabeth but by Metcalfe, who would have used the woman until all such finances had been exhausted. Perhaps as Elizabeth Nicholson walked from the courtroom that day in June 1904, it suddenly dawned on her what a fool she had been, an extremely fortunate fool.

7

THE MYSTERY OF THE MUTINEER'S DEATH

THE KILLING OF PERCY TOPLIS AT PLUMPTON, JUNE 1920

Percy Toplis was a ruthless, cold-blooded killer, and a cad into the bargain. The murder normally associated with Toplis occurred outside the Cumbrian boundaries, but so intriguing are the circumstances and so deep is the Cumbrian involvement, especially that of the Cumberland police, that the case seems to warrant inclusion here. We still do not know to this day who killed Percy Toplis.

Toplis served as a private in the British Army, and was in 1920 stationed at Bulford camp, near Salisbury. A soldier who found it difficult to accept discipline, he was frequently called before the station authorities and served 'jankers' (internal service punishment, ranging from imprisonment to carrying out menial tasks such as toilet cleaning etc) for his breaches of discipline. After one punishment he decided that enough was enough, and Toplis deserted.

On 25th April 1920, a taxi driver was found murdered in Southampton, a relatively short distance from Bulford. His grey Darracq taxi was missing. The driver had been shot in the back of the head and an examination of the bullet found in the brain indicated that the weapon was a revolver of the type used by service personnel.

The police made enquiries at local service camps and information was received that one Percy Toplis was

Percy Toplis – army deserter, murderer and uncommon thief.

missing, as too was his revolver. Along with Toplis was another soldier by the name of Fallows. A short time later the pair were seen in the missing taxi, in Swansea!

Fallows was to return to Bulford and later told how Toplis had encouraged him to assist in the theft of the car. Fallows declined to have anything more to do with Toplis and also claimed that he knew nothing of the murder of the taxi driver.

Percy Toplis went on the run and during the following months he was seen in London, Dundee and Aberdeen, always on the look-out for easy targets to steal from and to deceive. He shot two men who were looking for the person who had been sleeping rough in their barns close to the village of Tomintoul, Aberdeen.

Toplis could never settle anywhere. Some people believe in the old maxim 'Once a thief, always a thief', and certainly in the case of Percy Toplis this was true. Had he been able to stop himself from stealing money or food, then he would have been able to remain in one place for a reasonable length of time. Instead, all he did was go from bad to worse, stealing and conning his way from town to town.

On Sunday, 7th June 1920 he was making his way south from Carlisle. He was dressed in his usual soldier's uniform. It was very warm and he stopped to rest by a Wesleyan chapel off the main Carlisle to London road (the A6) between Low and High Hesket. At this time, the whole country was on the look-out for Percy Toplis, who had been identified as an extremely violent and dangerous man, especially after the shootings in Scotland.

Police Constable Alfred Fulton, whose police officer uncle had been shot dead in the execution of his duty at Plumpton in 1885 by the Netherby Burglars, was a keen officer with some 13 years service in the Cumberland force. He came across the soldier resting by the chapel and asked for identification. At no point did he believe that the young man with whom he conversed was Toplis. The soldier produced identification which gave his name as John Henry Thompson. He said that he was making his way back to Catterick garrison, absent without leave rather than a deserter. Fulton fell for the lies, and feeling some pity for the 23 year old, told him to get on his way otherwise the punishment would be greater the longer he delayed his return.

On returning home Fulton was met by his wife, who told her husband that she had seen a man who fitted the

70

description of the infamous Percy Toplis, walking along the main road towards Penrith. It suddenly dawned upon the policeman that the soldier he had earlier spoken with was in fact Britain's most wanted man!

Fulton raised the alarm and went in search of the man. He knew he could not have gone far so first visited High Hesket. Ahead he saw the man disappear into some undergrowth by St Mary's church. Fulton followed and told him to come out. Toplis stepped out from behind a bush, in his hand a pistol which was aimed directly at the policeman's head. 'If it is Toplis you are after, I am your man. I had to shoot that lot in Tomintoul, and if you carry on being a bad lad I will have to shoot you. Now throw away your handcuffs and truncheon.' Fulton did as he was told and as Toplis disappeared back into the wooded area, he turned to Fulton and shouted, 'You must be the smartest lawman in England.' With that he waved an almost fond farewell to the officer.

The chase was now well and truly on. Some 150-plus police officers from Cumberland were detailed for immediate duty, among them an unofficial volunteer in the form of Norman de Courcy Parry, the son of the county's Chief Constable. The young Parry, aged just 22, one year younger than the country's number one quarry, armed himself with a small Belgian automatic, a souvenir from the war.

The Cumberland force surrounded the immediate area where Toplis was last seen, while a number of men in plain clothes were told to drive around the main routes in a car. Parry went out on his motorcycle in the hope of locating Toplis before anyone else. He did, close to Plumpton crossroads.

Parry stopped his bike, pretending it had broken down. Toplis had changed his appearance and was now wearing civilian clothing and a trilby hat. No sooner had Parry seen him than the plain clothes officers drove past

71

and also identified him. For a few minutes there was pandemonium as the officers in the car found themselves unable to stop as the civilian driver panicked in fear of a shoot-out!

Parry gave them the thumbs-up as they passed, a signal that this was the man they sought. Percy Toplis was bemused by the strange carry-on taking place before him, although he was suspicious of the stranger on the motorbike now immediately across the road from him.

'Who are those men, and what the hell are they up to?' Toplis asked Parry. 'I think they are joyriding.' 'Why did you give the thumbs-up signal to them?' 'I know a couple of them and hoped they would stop to give me a hand with my bike.'

Toplis told Parry to get his bike fixed and clear off. He then continued to walk slowly in the direction of Romanway Farm rose garden, where, unbeknown to him, the police lay in ambush. Parry followed and was about 23 yards behind.

Close to St John the Evangelist church, Plumpton, the ambush opened up. Two plain clothes officers leapt out from behind a stone wall and opened fire. Toplis turned on his heel and began to run, though every so often he would turn, crouch and return fire. Parry was close behind the two main police gunmen, who were quickly closing in on the wanted man. Toplis suddenly crouched down and slumped forward, clutching his chest as he rolled down a bank. He was fatally wounded and died there and then.

That was the end of the matter, you might think, a reasonably straightforward affair. The inquest verdict was that the outlaw had died from bullets fired by police officers in fear of their own lives, justifiable homicide. Toplis was buried in Penrith, Cumberland in a pauper's grave.

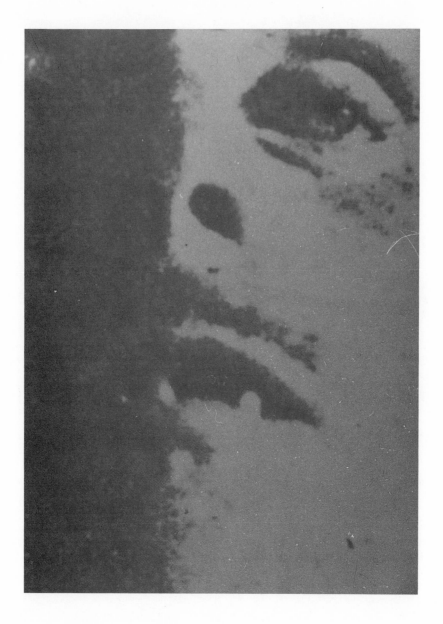

Percy Toplis, post mortem.

The roadside verge where Percy Toplis met his death.

Interest in the case never really died and was revived by the television dramatisation *The Monacled Mutineer*. In 1978 Norman de Courcy Parry was interviewed on television about the outlaw's last moments on earth. Parry told the interviewer that Toplis had in fact shot himself rather than be gunned down by the police. This was contrary to statements, both written and oral, made in 1920.

There were a number of local unofficial beliefs about how Percy Toplis died. These included the theory that he was killed unlawfully by a person or persons unknown who were also involved in the chase. If this was the case, then their actions would be officially classed as 'murder'. Speculation mounted when it was revealed that Parry dumped all of his weapons in the river Eamont, Penrith; not, it should be said, to disguise his part in the affair, but because he no longer wished to keep relics which reminded him of the war.

To this day the case is still discussed. Presumably, Parry himself was innocent, as he claimed that he never fired his gun. But then why carry it with him, why go in search of the villain, why join in the chase when bullets were being fired and put his own life at risk? Nothing has yet fully answered the riddle of who killed Percy Toplis.

8

BRUTAL SLAYING AT KIDHAM DUB

THE MURDER OF WAI-SHEUNG SIU AT KESWICK, JUNE 1928

The crime of murder, despite what the media may intimate, is rare, especially in more remote and sparsely populated counties such as Cumbria. Yet in 1928 a ghastly crime shocked the county, indeed the entire nation.

In America Chung Yi Miao, 28 years old, had met and married the daughter of a wealthy Chinese merchant, by the name of Wai-Sheung Siu. The girl was one year older than Chung and in what had been a whirlwind romance the couple found themselves flung together, passionately in love.

Wai-Sheung was a well travelled and shrewd businesswoman, who bought and sold Chinese art treasures all over the world. There can be no doubting that her new husband could count himself extremely lucky to be associated with such a financially well off family. Chung Yi Miao claimed to have studied and taken law degrees at Loyola University in Chicago, a fact which has never yet been substantiated, but one which certainly seems to have been accepted by his wife.

On 12th May 1928 the couple married in New York and set out on their honeymoon European voyage, heading first to Scotland. The pair had heard a great deal about Gretna Green and wished to visit the blacksmith's

Chung Yi Miao and Wai-Sheung Siu.

cottage. Having spent a short time in Scotland it was decided that they should spend a few days in the Lake District.

Travelling down from Scotland on Monday, 18th June

1928, they headed for the pleasant town of Keswick. Rooms were found at the nearby Borrowdale Gates Hotel, at the southern foot of Derwentwater. Checking into the hotel the couple were greeted by hotel staff who were genuinely thrilled to have two honeymooners from the other side of the world spending some time with them. Other guests congratulated them on their recent union and recommended places to visit in the area. The couple were not dissimilar to a pair of lovebirds, gazing into each other's eyes, and with permanent smiles seemingly etched upon their faces.

The following morning the couple went out for a walk, taking a stroll through the spectacular woodland around Derwentwater. Everywhere they went, people smiled and warmly acknowledged their presence. They returned to the Borrowdale Gates at around noon and had lunch before again leaving the hotel at about 2 pm. At some time around 4 pm Chung was seen walking back into the hotel reception, alone. He seemed quite relaxed and made his way to his room. Three hours later he emerged from his room and took dinner along with all the other guests; he was still alone.

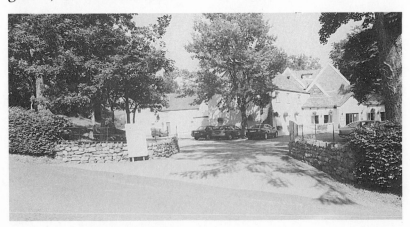

The Borrowdale Gates Hotel.

A guest on the next table asked where his wife was. 'It's rather cold, so she has gone to Keswick to buy some warm underclothes,' he replied. It was a reasonable explanation but Chung seemed uncomfortable when discussing the matter. The guest, believing that he was concerned as to her whereabouts, attempted to comfort him. 'I would not overly concern yourself with your wife's well being, she is a well travelled woman, a woman who knows how to look after herself. There are no problems here in the Lake District. She will be back soon, you wait and see.'

Chung volunteered that he had not gone with his wife as he had a slight head cold; she had told him to go back to the hotel and get some rest in a warm bed. He seemed rather anxious. A short time later, at 8.15 pm, the owner of the hotel sat with him and also asked where his good lady was. Once again he explained that she had gone to Keswick to purchase some warm underclothes. He said he had expected her to have returned by this time, and expressed his concern over her safety.

Miss Crossley (the hotel owner) told Chung that his wife had probably been having a good look around Keswick, and said that she would go to the bus terminus, which was by the post office, as a bus was expected at 9 pm. 'No, you need not bother yourself, my wife does not like to travel on a bus. She will return by private car. But thank you anyway.'

Miss Crossley felt sure that Wai-Sheung would be on the bus, so she left the hotel and went to the bus terminus. It was now around 9.15 pm. Chung suddenly made an appearance in the kitchen area of the hotel and asked a maid, Miss Holliday, where Miss Crossley was. The maid told him that she had gone to the bus stop to meet his wife. Chung asked, 'Where would she go to?' 'To the post office,' replied Holliday. 'Would she go to the place where they bathe?' was Chung's curious response. It was

79

The murder scene at Kidham Dub.

then explained where the post office was. Chung wandered off, apparently back to his room.

Wai-Sheung never did return to the Borrowdale Gates Hotel, for unbeknown to the other guests and staff, who were becoming anxious for her safety, she had already been found, murdered!

It was approximately 7.30 pm that same evening when local farmer Tom Wilson was out walking in the woods near Derwent Water. Seeing a brown sun umbrella he was curious as to who would be out at that time of night, especially in such cool conditions. The umbrella was opened, thus restricting his view of the bather sheltering beneath it next to a natural bathing pool known locally as Kidham Dub. Wilson wandered over to the pool and saw a woman lying on her back, knees drawn up and legs apart. Realising that something was wrong, he rushed to the body and saw that it was that of an Oriental woman, apparently dead.

Closer examination revealed that her skirt and underskirt had been pulled up around her hips, and that her underclothes were torn, clearly indicating some kind of sexual assault. Next to her left hand lay a white kid glove, peeled from the hand and still partially inside out. Wilson ran as fast as he could to Keswick to raise the alarm, and to summon the local police.

A short time after this discovery Miss Crossley informed the local police station of her concern for a guest who had failed to return. She provided a description and explained that the missing woman's husband was also a guest at the hotel. The police advised her that an officer would call round and that further enquiries would be necessary. However, Miss Crossley felt it curious that the officer receiving her call should ask several times as to the whereabouts of the husband.

It was 11 pm when Inspector Graham arrived in the foyer of the Borrowdale Gates Hotel. 'I am here on enquiries about a missing woman, I believe her husband is one of your guests?' Miss Crossley identified the guest and named his wife, totally unaware at this time that the police had located the woman. Inspector Graham, accompanied by other uniformed officers, knocked on Chung's room door. 'It is the police, I need to speak with you.' Chung was in bed and asked what they wanted. The police entered and immediately cautioned Chung, who was told to dress and then taken into police custody on suspicion of having caused his wife's death. Graham later recalled that he felt the performance put on by Chung, an act of emotional distress, was not a convincing one but clearly something he had enacted in his mind for several hours.

A search of his room was carried out and his overcoat and clothing worn that day were seized. Also taken were two undeveloped films, one of which contained a wrapped-up piece of silver paper in which were found a wedding ring and a diamond solitaire, identical to the one seen on the dead woman's finger the night before her death.

The following morning, Superintendent Barron arrived at Keswick police station to interview the prisoner. Having introduced himself and put the prisoner at some ease, he found himself wondering over an unusual outburst by Chung. 'This is terrible, my wife being assaulted, robbed and murdered, who would do such a thing?' Barron was to make further enquiries about this same conversation, but having spoken with all the officers who had spent some time with Chung, it was ascertained that none of them had mentioned the robbery. It was a damning piece of evidence, one which the defence counsel tried to disprove.

Chung told Barron that the bloodstains which would be found upon his overcoat were the result of an accident in New York, and were not recent. Again, it was an intimation that he knew blood had been spilled during his wife's murder.

A medical examination carried out on the body showed that Wai-Sheung had been severely beaten around the head and face, blood running from her ear, nose and mouth. Around her neck was a double loop of cord used to strangle her, the cause of death being asphyxiation. Despite appearances, there were no positive signs of sexual intercourse.

Forensic examination proved that the glove found at the scene had in fact been removed after the assault had taken place. Bloodstains showed that it had been peeled off by an outside source in a manner as to make it virtually impossible for the woman to have removed it herself. The wedding ring and solitaire which had been on her fingers at all times up until the crime occurred, were now missing.

Cord similar to the type used to strangle Wai-Sheung

was found in Chung's hotel room and in the kitchen area of the hotel, which had been accessible to all guests. However, it has to be said that the cord was in fact a different colour to that found on the body. Chung was charged with his wife's murder and held in custody.

He was brought to trial at Carlisle Assizes before the trial judge, Mr Justice Humphreys. It was 22nd November 1928 and the city of Carlisle had seen nothing like it. Yes, it had seen its fair share of murderers being executed, but nothing like the press and media circus which accompanied this case. Which, it has to be said, made it something of a farce. English Street, Botchergate and Bank Street were packed with curiosity seekers attempting to get a look at the prisoner. Reporters spoke with anyone who could tell a tale about murder in the county, comparing this crime with some of the county's other, more chilling incidents.

The case for the prosecution was quite clear, although it is noticeable that every piece of evidence introduced was circumstantial. There was no direct proof of Chung's guilt, which he strongly denied throughout the three day hearing.

The defence did everything within its power to defy the prosecution's case. Mr Jackson, acting on behalf of the prisoner, brought into question Chung's command of the English language. He also pointed out that Chung spoke with a lisp, which hardly enhanced his pronunciation. Thus he claimed that the hotel maid who said that Chung had asked if Miss Crossley had gone 'to the place where they bathe', had misheard him. Jackson claimed that Chung actually said, 'Has she gone to the place where people take the bus?' The maid accepted that she may well be wrong, a positive factor for the defence.

Next, Mr Jackson said that Superintendent Barron was also wrong, when the senior officer believed Chung to have said 'robbed and murdered'. Chung had actually said 'rudely murdered'. The Assistant Chief Constable refused to accept this suggestion. 'I know what he said, so do others. I am not mistaken.'

As if this was not sufficient doubt, next came the sighting of two mysterious strangers, two Orientals. Chung claimed that he had first noticed these people following him and his bride in Glasgow, then in Edinburgh, and finally in Grange, next to Derwent Water. He had no idea who these people were but knew them to be up to no good. Chung further explained that his wife was of a flighty nature. She enjoyed showing off her jewellery and flirting with men. He felt this a dangerous pastime and had warned her against the perils of such actions.

In an attempt to explain how he came to be in possession of his wife's jewellery, the same jewellery which Chung so blatantly stated that his wife was fond of showing off, he stated: 'After my warning, and the sighting of the two strange Orientals, my wife decided that I was right, so she hid them in a spool of Kodak film for safekeeping. This she placed in her suitcase on top of the wardrobe in our room.' Once again, it was a perfectly reasonable explanation.

The prosecution satisfactorily questioned the sightings of these Oriental strangers. The only reports of any credence were of the prisoner and his wife when she was alive. None of the others tallied. It was also brought into evidence that Chung was in fact not a man of any financial means, he had married his wife because of her wealth, and nothing else.

Also introduced was the fact that Wai-Sheung had had an operation on 25th May 1928, because of a physical condition which prevented her from having sexual intercourse. The possibility was that Chung had become sexually frustrated because of this, and had tried to force her, carrying out a vicious attack when failing to do so.

The *Illustrated Police News* reports the murder in June 1928.

Afterwards, it was claimed, he staged the entire incident so as to take the appearance of a robbery!

The judge carried out his summing up of the case on the third day. The jury were instructed that if they held any doubts as to the prisoner's guilt, then he should be found not guilty. However, if they felt he was lying and had invented much of his evidence, 'then he is clearly guilty of not telling the truth of the matter and you may well say, knows more than he is prepared to tell us in this courtroom.' The jury retired for just one hour. When they returned their spokesman stood up and pronounced their result as 'Guilty of murder'.

Chung was given the opportunity of responding to the charge before punishment was prescribed. 'I am innocent. I have not been given the opportunity to put my point of view forward to the jury, or the judge in this case. The last word I have to say is this, you say, how clever he is, now you have tried my life and the verdict is I am guilty. I ask you this. If I did that, I must be very nervous. Now you see, I am not nervous.' It was a remarkable outburst, but not one which was unusual, as condemned prisoners often verbally attacked their counsel and the jury. Mr Justice Humphreys, clearly unimpressed by the statement, duly sentenced him to death.

An appeal was lodged and heard by the Lord Chief Justice, Mr Justice Avory accompanied by Mr Justice Acton. Chung sacked his counsel and offered his own case. Incredibly, his main course of appeal was on the grounds that he had not been given a fair trial, and that the initial trial judge and jury had been prejudiced against him. He introduced new witnesses who claimed to have seen different Orientals in the Keswick area, but this was hardly sufficient to prove that they had followed the couple halfway round the world in order to commit murder!

No point of law had been raised in the hearing and the evidence introduced was not influential upon the case, thus the appeal was dismissed. Chung was again furious, although on this occasion he simply broke down in tears. He was handcuffed and taken to a waiting police car which conveyed him from the London law courts to Strangeways prison in Manchester.

Chung Yi Miao was executed on 6th December 1928, exactly 16 days after his appeal had been examined and dismissed. He allegedly confessed to the crime before being put to death, telling a newspaper reporter that he killed his wife because of 'religious feelings; in South China there is reverence for ancestors. Thereby any man who cannot father a son to revere his memory is accursed.'

Right or wrong, we shall never know. Newspapers had a terrible habit of printing alleged confessions, though few, if any, honestly existed. Many were third hand, bought and sold by those eager to make a few pounds from their association with prisoner or victim. The sad fact of the matter is that Chung must have killed his wife. After all, there is no other reasonable explanation, is there?

9

HANGED BY
THE NECK

THE MURDER OF ALAN WEST AT SEATON, APRIL 1964

Seaton, in west Cumbria, is the largest village in the county, with over 5,000 inhabitants. Its origins can be traced back many years and it was for a long time a mining community with many of its original inhabitants working at the brickworks or down the mine.

John Alan West was a locally employed west Cumbrian, who had lived in the same house, 28 Kings Avenue, Seaton for 25 years. In 1964, this house was one of six in a peaceful cul-de-sac, backing on to open fields. The houses were basic, semi-detached properties, box like, with the main entrance door to the side of the premises. West had lived alone at number 28 since the death of his mother in 1963.

At the age of 55, Alan West (his preferred name, although he was also known as Jack) had been regularly employed by Lakeland Laundries since the age of 20. He had started as a van driver, collecting and delivering to hotels, schools and other company clients. He was a hard working man and by 1964 had earned an office job, without the rigours of physical exertion. This suited him better, although he did enjoy being his own man when out and about in the van. In 1954 after 25 years with the company, Alan had received a gold watch complete with personalised inscription on its rear casing. Alan was extremely proud of the watch.

Alan West's home in King's Avenue, Seaton.

Living alone had not been easy since his mother's death, although Alan had plenty of friends. He was a regular at the Great Clifton British Legion, but he preferred to be home and in bed by 10 pm each evening. Loneliness can often create routine, it certainly had with Alan West. Everything was done like clockwork, somewhat to the amusement of his neighbours.

On the night of 6th April 1964 Alan West's routine was broken. His next door neighbours, the Fawcetts, returning home from the local club noticed that though it was after 10 pm, Alan's living room light was on. At 11 pm, when they went to bed, it was still on.

It was around 3 am when the Fawcetts awoke with a start. A dull and continual thudding noise had aroused them from their slumbers. Both sat up in bed and listened intently as the noises continued, but not to the same degree. They seemed to be coming from Alan's house next door. What on earth could he be doing at this hour of the morning?

89

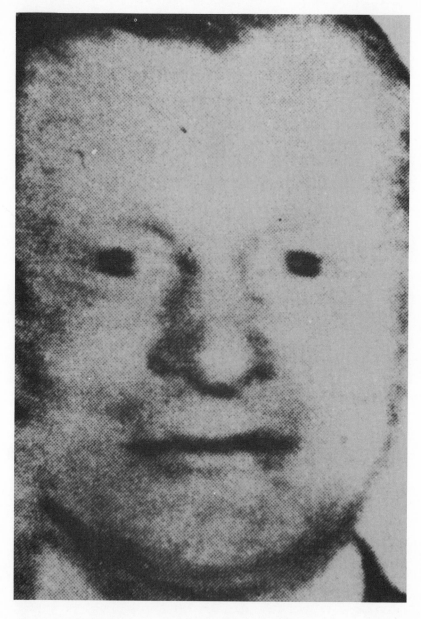

Alan West – victim.

Unable to believe that Alan would make such a row, Joseph Fawcett looked out into the street. From the illumination of next door's garden he could see that at least one upstairs and one downstairs light were on at number 28. It was all very confusing.

The noise of a car door slamming and an engine suddenly bursting into life was not unusual by any standards, however this engine was clearly being pushed to its limits, revving ferociously. Lights came on all around the cul-de-sac as locals peered out into the darkness to see what was happening. Suddenly there was the crunch of a car being engaged in gear, quickly followed by the squeal of tyres, and the car was heard leaving the near vicinity at what sounded like a fast rate.

The Fawcetts dressed and went out into the street. They were accompanied by another neighbour by the name of Walter Lister. The trio went to Alan West's home to check that everything was all right. The lights were on but no reply to their knocking was received. Lister ran back to his home and telephoned the police. Although suspicious, there was nothing to show that anything sinister had actually occurred at that time. Thus, at 3.30 am police patrol vehicle 'Bravo 24', manned by Sergeant Bill Park and Constable John Rodgers, was instructed to call at 28 Kings Avenue, Seaton, where neighbours had become suspicious of noises emanating from the house.

All the doors to the house were locked, but Joe Fawcett told the sergeant that a spare key was kept in a nailbox in the garage. This was found and used to open the front door. As the door swung open both men saw a pair of bare legs and a pool of blood. Fawcett collapsed in a heap and was immediately attended to by PC Rodgers. The sergeant closed the front door and noted the scene before him. 'A body lay on the floor at the foot of the stairs. The body was on its back, dressed only in a shirt and vest. The body was at an angle to the staircase. There were obvious severe head injuries. There was a large amount of blood on the floor, and the man was obviously dead. There was also quite a lot of blood on the staircase, and it appeared that a struggle had taken place.'

A thorough search of the premises was made to ensure that no one else was there. The sergeant instructed PC Rodgers to stand guard by the main side door, and not to allow anyone in without his permission. At 3.45 am Sergeant Park returned to his car and used the police radio. 'Can we have a senior officer here, 28 Kings Avenue, Seaton, I have a sudden death in suspicious circumstances, we need a doctor, and the CID.'

Dr Ian MacLeod, a local practitioner, attended the scene and made a brief external examination of the body, before declaring 'life extinct'.

Inspector John Gibson attended the scene at 4.30 am. He found on the floor of the living room a piece of piping, measuring approximately one foot in length. This was covered in rubber and had been wrapped in a pair of pyjama trousers. He also found a steel bolt on the fourth tread of the stair. On the upstairs landing was a metal poker, and a set of lower dentures which were the property of Alan West.

While all this was taking place the wheels of officialdom, which surrounds all such major enquiries, were slowly turning. After several telephone calls Detective Chief Superintendent Alan Roberts of Lancashire CID was appointed to head the investigation. This was the 37th such case he had been assigned as overall commander. He was a man with a superb detection record, and an officer who knew his success was down to the hard work of the officers on the ground, not just his own skills.

A raincoat was found in the main bedroom of the house. It was ascertained that this was not the property of the dead man, so whose was it? Inside one of the pockets were found a key and a medallion which bore the inscription 'G.O. Evans, July 1961'. The coat also revealed a piece of paper with a name and address upon it.

Enquiries were made at the address, in Preston, Lancashire. It transpired that a young girl by the name of O'Brien was the person named on the note. Police officers showed her the medallion which she at once identified as belonging to Gwynne Evans, a man she had met at her sister's house and with whom she had been out on a couple of occasions. The young girl further informed the police that Evans lodged with a man by the name of Peter Allen at 2 Clarendon Street, Preston.

Elsewhere, a stolen car had been located in Ormskirk, Lancashire. Fingerprints found within the vehicle belonged to two known criminals – Peter Allen and Gwynne Owen Evans! The liaison between the Lancashire and Cumberland and Westmorland forces was second to none; there had always been a good relationship between the two and now, when it was most necessary, it proved totally professional and allowed enquiries to proceed with the utmost expediency.

On Wednesday, 8th April 1964, Peter Allen was arrested on suspicion of theft of a motor vehicle. Gwynne Owen Evans was arrested on suspicion of murder, and conveyed to Workington police station. With Allen's prints being found alongside those of Evans in the stolen motor vehicle, and the time scale of the car's theft and discovery, it was clear that both men had to have been together on the night of Monday, 6th April 1964, probably in Seaton. Within 48 hours of the discovery of the murder, police had in custody two suspects from a separate county.

Among Evans' property was found a driver's licence which belonged to the owner of the stolen vehicle. 'I found it in Preston yesterday morning,' was his

93

Gwynne Owen Evans.

explanation. However, when confronted with a gold watch bearing the name 'J.A. West' he seemed lost for words. 'Yes, that watch was given to me by a man in Preston. I gave him £2 for it as he wanted petrol money,' he blurted out.

Gwynne Evans knew that his time was up, the evidence was stacked against him, and when he was told that the watch belonged to a man murdered in Seaton he volunteered a confession which immediately implicated Peter Allen and identified him as the killer.

Meanwhile, Detective Chief Superintendent Roberts was interviewing Allen at Workington police station, where Allen continually denied anything to do with the crime.

Then without warning he broke down and said, 'Alright, I will tell you about it, I will tell the whole flippin' world about it.' Roberts quickly reminded him that he was under caution. Allen continued: 'It started off as an innocent robbery. On Monday night at about 9.30 we went to a garage in Preston and pinched a car. I picked the wife and babies up but she didn't know what we was going on. We came up here and when we got here, Sandy got in (Sandy was a name used by Gwynne Owen Evans).

'We got here at 1.10. This bloke knew Sandy and Sandy said that he had money lying around. We parked the car in front of the roadworks. He went in and he came out for me about ten to three and I went in. Sandy told him that he wanted some fresh air and let me in without the chap knowing, but when he came downstairs he saw me so I hit him. Sandy had the bar and he gave it to me. Sandy put the lights out and I was hitting out blindly, I only had my fists until Sandy gave me the bar. I only hit him twice with it, and then gave it back to Sandy.

'I went upstairs to see if there was any loose cash, but there wasn't. There was a bunch of letters and two bank books in the drawer and I just grabbed the lot. The wife and children were asleep in the car.

'We went straight down the road towards Cockermouth. I threw my gloves out of the window. When we got to Windermere we ran out of petrol, but Sandy got some more. We went to Kendal and the wife cashed her family allowance and we went straight to Liverpool to see my mum.

'On the way back we dumped the car in a yard, a builder's yard near the bus depot. We got a bus back. Yesterday Sandy got two £5 notes from a bank in Liverpool. The wife went to the door with him, this was from West's account.

'When we got back I scrubbed my jeans and burned the letters I had grabbed. Sandy took the chap's watch and jacket and he left his own coat in the house. I'll tell you this, I'm glad you have found me. Sandy said it was an easy touch. Who am I to take a human life in my hands? All I wanted was a hundred pounds for a deposit on a house. I burned the shirt I was wearing.'

A further written statement differed slightly to this verbal confession, in which Allen claimed that he punched West as they confronted each other on the landing to the staircase. He then stated that Gwynne Evans struck the old man with the pipe, knocking him downstairs.

Nothing is ever that simple, particularly in a murder investigation when all evidence has to be checked again and again to ensure its accuracy. What had not been revealed at that point was that Alan West had died as a result of a stab wound which had 'nicked the lung, and penetrated the heart'. Yet Peter Allen made no mention of a knife!

During Evans' interview with the officer in charge of the case, he made the following comment without prompting. 'I don't know anything about a knife. I do not own a knife, I am a judo expert. It was Peter who did all the hitting.' The evidence was still being gathered by the murder squad but there were many ambiguities. For example, why did West have just his shirt and vest on? Why was Evans' raincoat in a bedroom? Why did Evans go in alone? Gwynne Owen Evans was to clarify these points, and many more.

Alan John West was a homosexual, who had in the past had many relationships, including with Gwynne Evans. On the night in question, Evans had gone to his home to ask for money. West had agreed to give him some, but not without first having sex, and he duly asked Evans to go to bed with him. It was at this point, with West undressed, that Allen entered the house. What was supposed to have happened was that Evans and West would be engaged in sex upstairs while Allen rifled through the downstairs rooms stealing anything of any value.

West had disturbed him and the assault took place at the top of the stairs, the pipe being wrapped in West's pyjama bottom by Evans. Basically, Allen had panicked and attacked West, and Evans had joined in to ensure that West was silenced.

The pair were charged with murder and stood trial at Workington Magistrates' Court. The case was then committed to Manchester Crown Court. The court case commenced on 19th June 1964 with both men pleading not guilty to murder. They gave evidence and again changed their stories, each blaming the other for the stabbing and for the murder. It was a farce – no honour amongst thieves here as both men lied through their teeth to implicate the other. The trial continued until Tuesday, 7th July 1964, when at 2.38 pm the jury returned a verdict of guilty of murder. Both men were sentenced to death.

Mr Lionel Lightfoot, the Under-Sheriff of Cumberland

All Communications
to be addressed to
G. L. G. LIGHTFOOT
UNDER SHERIFF

TEL. NOS. 88888-8
YOUR REF.:
MY REF.: GLSL

UNDER SHERIFF'S OFFICE
21 CASTLE STREET
CARLISLE

Dear Sir,

14th July 1964

re: 11115 Peter Anthony Allen

The above is a prisoner at H. M. Prison, Liverpool, who
was sentenced to death on 7th July for Capital Murder.

By reason of the fact that the offence took place in
Cumberland the High Sheriff of this County is charged with
the duty of making arrangements to carry out the sentence.

The prisoner has made an application for leave to Appeal
which application, I understand, will be heard on Monday 20th
July next.

In the event of the sentence being carried out I shall
be glad if you will let me know if you will undertake the
duties.   In view of the application for leave to Appeal, no
date has yet been fixed.

I enclose a stamped addressed envelope for your reply.

R. L. Stewart, Esq.,
2 Birchenlea Street,
CHADDERTON,
Lancs.

Yours faithfully,

Ghiwell Shinglepass

Robert Stewart's invitation to his final job.

sent letters to two individual hangmen: to Harry Allen,
requesting that he hang Evans at Manchester on a date to
be decided, and to Robert Stewart asking that he hang
Peter Allen at Liverpool.

Appeals against the convictions and sentencing were
lodged with the Home Office, all of which failed. A letter
was even sent to Her Majesty the Queen, who was at
Balmoral, requesting her intervention as Gwynne Evans
had a history of mental illness; the letter was forwarded
by Evans' mother! The Home Secretary denied any

reprieve and the Queen could not interfere with the course of the law.

At 8 am on the morning of 13th August 1964 Gwynne Owen Evans was executed at Manchester's Strangeways prison. Outside the prison walls all was quiet, not a soul murmured. Nobody showed the slightest interest in this man's demise. At Walton prison, Liverpool, at precisely the same time and date, Peter Allen was executed. A small group of people protested against the hanging outside the prison walls; not that they believed Allen was innocent, but they were part of the anti-capital punishment movement then gaining in influence. The campaign for the abolition of capital punishment worked. Gwynne Owen Evans and Peter Allen were the last two persons to officially hang in Britain.

10

THE END OF
THE ROAD

THE MANSLAUGHTER OF MARGARET HOGG, WAST WATER,
OCTOBER 1976

What to do with the body? Over the years different murderers have attempted all kinds of methods of disposal, from chopping them up and hiding them down the drains, to dissolving them in a vat of acid. It is without doubt that the disposal of the remains causes the greatest problem to any would-be killer.

Peter Hogg was a man faced with such a predicament. He lived with his 37 year old wife, Margaret, at Mead Road, Cranleigh, Surrey. The couple had two children, both boys, one aged eleven, the other six. Peter Hogg was some eleven years older than his wife and was employed as an airline pilot with Air Europe.

In 1973, while the couple were in Los Angeles, Margaret Hogg met another man who later became her lover. The man was also married with family responsibilities; he too lived in Surrey. The affair continued with Margaret literally flaunting the fact before her husband's eyes. At one point she even persuaded Peter to have a vasectomy, then afterwards announced that she was pregnant by her lover! She later suffered a miscarriage.

Despite this, Peter Hogg remained very much the gentleman, continuing to look after and raise the family. Hogg bought his wife a little restaurant near their home in a vain attempt to direct her spare time and interests

Peter and Margaret Hogg in happier times.

elsewhere. This simply encouraged Margaret to invite her lover there and allow him to eat for free! By 1976, matters were about to come to a head.

On the night of 17th October 1976, Margaret and Peter were involved in a rather nasty domestic altercation. Margaret had recently spent a week in a remote Dorset cottage, accompanied, of course, by her lover. She again taunted her husband with tales of how wonderful a man her lover was. Enough was enough, the normally mild mannered pilot snapped. He grabbed Margaret by the throat and gripped hard. He held this position for a short time, until Margaret fell to the floor, dead.

Hogg now faced a serious problem. Here he was in his pleasant home in Surrey with his wife dead at his feet. Peter Hogg was used to high pressure situations, and he had in fact thought about this very possibility, albeit he never truly expected that such a time would arrive.

What he needed was a good alibi. He at once

101

telephoned the headmaster of the Taunton boarding school where his eldest son was tutored. An appointment was made to see the headmaster the following day. Hogg then drove to the school, kept his appointment and told the headmaster that he was staying locally with a view to taking his son home with him the following morning, half term. The headmaster thanked Hogg for taking the trouble to inform him and said that this was acceptable.

Peter Hogg then jumped in his Alfa Romeo and drove the 400 plus miles to Cumbria. In the boot of his car was the body of his wife, wrapped in a polythene sheet, and a rubber dinghy. En route he stopped at roadworks and took some concrete blocks.

It was a black, cold night in Cumbria. Peter Hogg pulled up close to the shore of Wast Water, the county's most uninviting lake. At some places it is around 750 feet deep and can possess an eerie atmosphere on the most pleasant of days. Peter Hogg had no time to think about things that go bump in the night. He inflated the dinghy, removed his wife's body from the boot of the Alfa and weighted it down with concrete blocks. He then began to row to the centre of the lake.

The swell in Wast Water that night was bad and the tiny dinghy was tossed all over the place. Even worse, the dinghy was slowly filling with water as it spilled over the sides. Conditions were appalling, forcing Hogg to abandon his journey to the centre of the lake, and he was around 50 yards offshore when he manhandled the body of his wife overboard, and down into the murky depths. If everything went to plan, the body of Margaret Hogg would sink down to the lake's deepest area, thus ensuring that it would never be found. Hogg must have been quietly confident as he put the dinghy back into his car and drove to Taunton, where he collected his son.

The following day he put into operation the next part of his plan. He reported Margaret missing, informing the police that she had a lover and would in all probability be with him. Since, on this evidence, she was not a person who could be categorised as 'at risk', the police would not be overly concerned as to her whereabouts, as adults can generally look after themselves.

That was the end of the matter. Peter Hogg would probably have got away with his crime had it not been for the disappearance of another female in the Lake District. Veronique Marre failed to return to her home in France after a fell-walking holiday. Hotels were checked and her last known movements traced. It seemed possible that she had met with some kind of fatal accident whilst out on the fells, though why the body was proving so difficult to locate was another problem, especially with there being so many people in the area. Surely someone would have found her? Rescuers voiced the opinion that she had probably drowned, possibly in Wast Water as she was known to have been in the vicinity of the village of Wasdale. A search of the lake by a police diving team initially proved fruitless, until the arrival of a local sub aqua enthusiast who informed the officer in charge of a strange discovery he had made within the lake some three months earlier. The diver had seen a polythene sheet anchored to the bottom of the lake in about 100 feet of water.

The bundle was located and removed. It was not the body of 21 year old Veronique Marre. This corpse wore a wedding ring: inside the ring was the inscription 'Margaret, November 15, 1963 – Peter'. The mystery of the unknown corpse was publicised on television and in all the national newspapers. An anonymous call was received by police in Surrey telling officers to investigate the disappearance of Margaret Hogg in 1976. The caller had been female. Margaret's dental charts were sent to the police headquarters at Penrith; they matched those of the body found in Wast Water. On

5th March 1984 Peter Hogg was arrested on suspicion of murder.

He was tried at the Old Bailey in March 1985 and was found guilty of manslaughter, the jury believing that it had not been his deliberate intention to kill his wife. He was jailed for four years. Incidentally, the body of Veronique Marre has never been found.

Peter Hogg had been unfortunate not to get his wife's body that little bit further out into Wast Water. Although the crime did not actually occur within Cumbria, the county played an important role in this sinister affair, proving that even within its remote countryside, the perfect crime does not exist.

11

THE BUTLER DID IT!

THE MURDERS OF MARY COGGLE AND DONALD HALL
AT NEWTON ARLOSH, DECEMBER 1977 – JANUARY 1978

In time honoured tradition and with true dramatic style, the subject of this case was indeed the butler. A man of few if any principles, other than to line his own pockets with other people's property, he is perhaps one of the most despicable murderers of the modern era.

Archibald Hall was born in June 1924 in Glasgow, the son of an industrious and honest Post Office employee. His family upbringing was strict where manners and gentlemanly conduct were concerned, thus making him outwardly a pleasant and likeable young man.

As a teenager he took to stealing from the elderly. An old woman who lived close to his family home (in a block of flats) had taken to young Hall. In return, Archie would spend as much time as possible with the woman, cleaning for her and generally maintaining what appeared a genuine friendship. Everyone spoke of how courteous and helpful he was, so different in personality and ideals to other youngsters of his age group.

A short time later the old lady died; not, it must be said, in suspicious circumstances. Her death was a genuine one, her elderly and weak frame could simply take no more. For a while it seemed that Archie was devastated by the loss, but his grief was short-lived as he moved on to his next ploy. When relatives of the dead woman came to clear her flat they found a trunk full of money which she had been hiding for many years. Unbeknown to anyone at that time, Archibald Hall had been helping himself to some of this cash! Hence the regular visits.

He may have got away with that one, but his early criminal career was to be cut short in 1941 when he was found guilty of theft and sentenced to a short jail sentence, aged just 17. Upon his release he continued with his criminal activities, although he now turned to housebreaking.

Twelve months later he was again jailed. At this time the Home Office examined all convicted youngsters in an attempt to identify why offenders were becoming increasingly younger. The psychiatrist examining Hall declared him to be mentally unstable. Despite this, he was released from custody and once again resumed his criminal activities. In 1944 he was jailed for two years, on a further housebreaking charge. By 1946 he began to concentrate his activities on London, where the population was greater, with bigger and easier targets. In 1947 he was charged with burglary and forgery, when he stole cheques during one such raid and tried to cash them. The defence asked that some 51 other offences be taken into consideration; incredibly, he was jailed for just two years!

The ever increasing amount of time Hall was spending in prison did little to deter him, indeed it simply supplemented his knowledge of criminal activities. Hall believed that he could commit greater, more enterprising crimes than those who surrounded him. He regarded everyone as an idiot, a gullible fool ready to believe and accept anything or anyone they saw as an equal. Sadly, this perception was proved correct on more than one occasion.

In 1951 he found employment in Stirlingshire as a butler with a wealthy family. While they were away on holiday, he loaned out their Bentley, dressed in his employer's finest clothes, and went to a Royal garden party. He successfully deceived several persons at the party and stole from a Mrs Esta Henry!

Suspicion fell on him when police enquiries into his antecedents revealed that he was little more than a common thief; already a few local people had expressed their anxiety about the new man in the village. The local police inspector confronted Hall (who also passed himself off as 'Roy Fontaine'). Hall admitted to his criminal past but told the officer that he was starting a new, rehabilitated life. The inspector had no alternative but to ensure that his employers were aware of his past. They believed Hall's story of rehabilitation, but despite this the butler felt that things were growing a little too hot for his liking and elected to resign and leave the area.

In the few years of freedom which followed, Hall took to travelling the length and breadth of Britain. He could easily pass himself off as gentry and his favourite deception, simply because it was so easy, was to turn up at five star hotels in a large limousine. He would flaunt his fake affluence and order only the very best. This act would continue for several days before he would be up and off, literally disappearing overnight.

It is alleged that on one occasion he discoloured his skin with fruit juice, dressed in Arab regalia and arrived at a hotel in a Rolls-Royce. The hotel manager bent over backwards to please his Eastern guest. Hall then told the manager to send the best local jewellers to his room with some of their wares. The tradesmen duly arrived to find that, for religious reasons, the Arab could not greet them face to face, all contact had to be made through a door. Foolishly, the jewellers passed various valuables to the unseen Arab. The door closed and there were a few minutes of silence before the jewellers decided to see what was happening. They found the adjoining room empty, and on the floor lay some cast off Arab clothing!

On another occasion he conned his way into the Mayor of Torquay's civic reception, and was permitted to wear the chain of office! He got a free meal and VIP treatment.

Hall was a natural, he could even trick other criminals who knew full well that he was little more than a cheat and a liar. In 1956 he was jailed for offences which amounted to some 30 years' custodial sentencing. Once inside he played the ideal prisoner, pleasant and well behaved. Because of this he was given the privilege of temporary release to attend his father's funeral. True to his word (for once in his life) he returned to Parkhurst on time. Incredibly, taking into account good behaviour, he was released after just seven years!

Upon his release in 1963 he took up work as a butler at a house in Mayfair, London. A short time later he obtained the job as butler to Sir Charles Clore, but was asked to resign after just five days in the position. Again, a local police officer had warned the household of their new butler's murky past.

The following year he was jailed for ten years, having resumed his illegal pastimes, but he managed to escape from custody, before being recaptured after further crimes in 1966. He was sentenced to a further five years, to add to the ten outstanding from the time of his escape. In 1972 he was sent to a hostel in Preston, where he met and married one Mary Coggle. It will come as no surprise to learn that he was back in jail by the end of 1973, where he remained until 1977.

Archie left prison declaring that he was finished with 'serving time'. He told warders that he was a reformed character and needed a well earned rest. He managed to find employment, again as a butler, this time in Waterbeck, Dumfries, Scotland. Also employed there was another ex-con, by the name of David Wright, who was an out and out thief. Wright placed Hall's position in jeopardy with his foolish activities, committing several crimes which the butler had to cover up in fear of his own past again coming to light. Eventually, with the mistress of the household away, Hall took Wright shooting in the fields, and shot him dead. He then buried him beneath a pile of stones.

After a reasonable run of good fortune, Hall's employer sacked him after an enlightening conversation about his criminal background with the local constable. Hall was upset by this but was no doubt overjoyed about leaving Scotland and his first murder victim behind him.

Returning to London, he tricked his way into a wealthy ex-MP's home and got the job of butler. Mr Walter Travers Scott-Elliott was rich, 82 years old, and not as shrewd as he undoubtedly once was. Hall was reunited with Mary Coggle and one Michael Kitto in a London public house. Kitto was himself a criminal who had recently stolen a hefty sum from a public house where he had worked as a barman. The trio then planned the deception which would see them take much of the Scott-Elliotts' fortune.

A few days later Hall met with Kitto and again the men consumed a great amount of alcohol. 'Old Ma Elliott is away tonight, I will take you to the house and show you round while Walter sleeps,' said Hall to his new-found friend. The pair returned to the house and crept around as the unsuspecting Scott-Elliott slept.

'This is his wife's room,' said Hall as he pushed open Mrs Scott-Elliott's bedroom door. To his horror, there she stood. Archie Hall apologised for the 'mistake' but his mistress was not about to have any of it and screamed her annoyance at him. In order to silence her the pair leapt upon the defenceless woman, forced her back onto the bed and suffocated her with a pillow. With Mrs Scott-Elliott dead they then had to get rid of the body.

An elaborate plot was hatched which saw the pair drug her husband and disguise Mary Coggle as his wife. This done the group then drove to a rented cottage in Newton Arlosh, Cumberland. Poor Walter Scott-Elliott hardly knew what was happening; he thought the woman next to him on the back seat of the car driving north was his wife. Little did he know that his wife's body was wrapped in a blanket in the boot of the car.

The following day the group drove to Perthshire, and along the route buried Dorothy Scott-Elliott in remote countryside. That night they stayed in a hotel at Blair Athol, Perthshire. Walter Scott-Elliott had no idea that his wife was dead. The old man was still heavily drugged, unable to think for himself.

On 14th December 1977, Walter Scott-Elliott was murdered in a lonely clump of trees in countryside close to Edinburgh, where his remains were buried in a shallow grave consisting of wood, rocks and leaves. The murderous trio returned to Newton Arlosh.

In Cumberland, Mary Coggle insisted upon keeping a mink coat which had belonged to Dorothy Scott-Elliott. Archie Hall told her that it would lead to their downfall, there were to be no connections between them and the dead couple. A fight broke out and Hall struck Mary Coggles over the head with a poker. He then placed a plastic bag over her head and tied it around her neck, until she breathed no more. Mary was dumped beneath a concrete pipe subway alongside the A74 to the north of Carlisle. Four murders already committed – nothing could now stop Archibald Hall, and it seems that at no point did he ever feel concerned over his desperate position. Even he must have realised that you could not go about indefinitely killing people and dumping their bodies in the countryside.

Over the next week or so Hall and Kitto raided the Scott-Elliotts' possessions and made a considerable amount of money from their sale. Christmas was spent with Hall's family; Michael Kitto was now very much part of Hall's life!

Both Hall and Kitto returned to Newton Arlosh after Christmas. This time they had with them Archie's brother, Donald Hall. He was something of a sexual deviant with previous convictions for sexual offences against children. Donald was a pathetic excuse of a human being, slow, and lacking any intelligence he was hardly likely to find himself in any form of employment. Similarly, he would be of no use to Archie or Kitto.

Donald seemed to do little else but agitate his two companions, putting his nose in where others would maintain silence. The pair decided that he already knew too much. He was rendered unconscious with a chloroform-soaked rag, and drowned in the bath tub.

Donald's body was placed in the boot of their car, a Ford Granada running on false number plates. The two men left Cumberland and headed for the North East, and Berwick. There they stayed at the Blenheim House Hotel, and attempted a deception upon the hotel manager, running up a hefty bar bill and requesting that it be added to their total accommodation bill. The manager was suspicious and called the local police who checked out the guests' car. The registration plates belonged to a Ford Escort and the tax disc to another vehicle. The police arrested Hall and Kitto on suspicion of theft.

At Berwick police station Archie Hall escaped from custody through an open toilet window but was quickly recaptured. The Ford Granada was searched and the body of Donald Hall discovered in the boot. With this evidence confronting them both Hall and Kitto confessed to their grisly list of murders.

At the subsequent trial, Kitto was sentenced to 15 years' imprisonment, Hall to life, without parole. If only such a sentence had been passed several years earlier when it was known that Hall was a continual offender, perhaps murder would not have been added to his list of convictions. Yet in reality the system cannot be blamed for the crimes of Archibald Hall. He was one of life's unfortunates who wanted what he could not achieve, wealth. Such avarice cost him dearly, although it cost five others a great deal more.

12

A NIGHTMARE AT THIEFSIDE

THE MURDER OF MICHELLE PAGE AT CALTHWAITE, OCTOBER 1987

The A6 trunk road has throughout the years received more than its fair share of notoriety. Running from London to Carlisle in the north of England, it was once the main route for travellers of all types, be they holidaymakers, haulage companies, or murderers! Perhaps the most infamous A6 incident was the Hanratty case, which occurred in the south of the country, near Bedford.

For centuries, this ancient route through Cumberland was ideal bandit country and many a highwayman used it as a base. The woodland and sparsely inhabited surrounding countryside made escape easy. One place which was favoured by the highwaymen was between Carlisle and Penrith on what is now the A6. Here travellers faced robbery which would undoubtedly involve the use of physical violence. Eventually, after many years, the area became synonymous with the highwaymen, and was referred to as 'Thiefside'. Once the authorities realised there was a recurring problem upon this route, sentries were posted to keep watch for any ambush. The highwaymen caught and tried would be executed on unofficial gallows to the east of the village of Calthwaite, along with sheep stealers and poachers.

Thus the name 'Thiefside' still remains in Calthwaite.

The gallows have long since disappeared, but the legend of many a notorious highwayman and despicable desperado lives on. In 1987 an horrific crime occurred within this very community. Long before the final act occurred however, events taking place elsewhere fashioned what was to become one of the county's most disturbing crimes.

Michael Derek Hearne was, in 1977, a well respected businessman who ran a furniture factory in Rawtenstall, Lancashire. The business was not hugely successful but provided sufficient funds for him and his teenage daughter to live in comfort. Mrs Hearne was no longer with them, but the pair had grown used to this and were quite happy together. As can be the case, however, the sudden involvement of a third party can cause so much intrusion, so much trouble, as to alter the course of people's lives. For the Hearnes that intruder, that third party, was a 16 year old girl named Michelle Page.

Michelle had recently moved into the Rawtenstall area after losing her father, who had passed away a short time earlier. The girl became friendly with Michael Hearne's daughter and was soon introduced to Michael, who felt some sympathy for the child. She was invited to move into the Hearne household to act as housekeeper, Michael offering to pay her a reasonable wage for carrying out day to day chores.

Initially things were reasonably straightforward, but life tends to throw in the odd hiccup to create disharmony. Michelle was 34 years her employer's junior, yet the occasional lasting glance indicated that both felt more than genuine friendship for each other. It was not too long before Hearne was actively involved with Michelle. Hearne believed, blindly, that he was enjoying a two-sided relationship; love is blind, but Hearne was just plain foolish. The adage 'There is no fool like an old fool' was never as apt as in this instance.

Slowly but surely Michael Hearne found his life crumbling around him, yet he ignored every one of his business principles which had served him so well in the past. Michelle was given money as and when she wanted it; a car, clothes, holidays, there was no end to his gratitude as Hearne desperately attempted to keep her with him.

Worse was to come. Michelle was still growing up and she needed to be with people of her own age group; there was a string of younger lovers and relationships. Michael was aware of these and did not wish to interfere with her happiness, still content in the knowledge that she would at the end of the evening come home to him.

As if this was not sufficient for him to deal with, his entire furniture business all but collapsed around him when he lost £60,000 in a fraud which had been planned for some time. Everyone who knew him could see that he no longer held any interest in his business, and he was easy prey for the rogue.

Eventually, in 1982, he sold his business and, to get away from local gossip, the pair moved from Lancashire to Cumbria. A pig farm was bought, but was not to his liking and was sold after three years when the pair moved to Thiefside Cottage, Calthwaite. The scene was set for disaster. It was clear that someone would eventually be hurt within the relationship, and it seemed likely to be Hearne, who had given up everything he owned to keep Michelle.

One of Michelle's favourite pastimes in the Cumbrian countryside was to watch the grass track racing which took place most weekends in the surrounding area. Her interest introduced her to many new friends and acquaintances, including Harold Graham Martin, a 27 year old man who took to her warm and pleasant character. The couple became friends and before too long were lovers; having first met in September 1986, they were engaged in January 1987.

As for Michael Hearne, he was virtually bankrupt, his money frittered away through his indulgence of a young girl who no longer wanted anything to do with him. Michelle had been spending more and more time away from her live-in lover, whose home she had shared for the past ten years. He had nothing more to offer her, whereas Harold Martin, she once told a friend, was 'a really nice bloke. I feel good when I am with him, I think he likes me as well.'

The majority of the villagers of Calthwaite had naturally assumed that Michelle was Hearne's daughter, but slowly the stories and whispers began to circulate in the rural community. Worse was to come. The relationship over, Michelle moved out and that, one would have hoped, would be the end of the matter. Hearne was told that she and Harold were to be married on 21st May 1988 and this news finally convinced him that there was no going back, it was all over between him and his young lover, now aged 25.

In an attempt to regain some form of normality, the 60 year old man, who spent day after day alone in Thiefside Cottage, took up work selling beefburgers from a portable caravan on the A6, in a lay-by close to the Calthwaite junction.

It was a sad and frustrating waste of a life. The hours spent by the side of the A6 allowed Hearne the time to think, to plot, to plan his revenge. Quite simply, he had lost the ability of rational thought where Michelle Page was concerned. Matters were made worse by the news that Michelle was now pregnant.

Michael Hearne contacted Harold Martin and asked him if he would help get his car through its MOT. Harold, being a genuine enough chap, agreed to do so and collected the vehicle. On the night of Thursday, 1st

Thiefside Cottage, Calthwaite.

October 1987 both Harold and Michelle visited Thiefside Cottage in order to return the car to Hearne; Harold was pleased to tell him that the car had passed.

Hearne was polite and pleasant and offered a cup of tea to his visitors. Without wishing to appear rude the pair had no alternative but to accept his offer, as Hearne scurried out of the sitting room and into the kitchen to put the kettle on. Harold and Michelle were a little uncomfortable, but perhaps they felt it was a chance to lay to rest any animosity.

Within seconds, such thoughts were quickly forgotten, forever banished from both young minds. Michael Hearne calmly walked back into the sitting room brandishing a shotgun, which he had bought a short time earlier for the princely sum of £100. Without further explanation he let loose a shot into Michelle's stomach. She fell backwards onto the floor, clearly in great distress. Shocked, yet acting instinctively, Harold Martin flew at

117

Hearne, knocking him to the ground before wrenching the shotgun from his grasp. He broke it open and removed the unused cartridges from Hearne's possession, thus preventing its further use. The weapon was then flung outside the cottage front door.

Hearne was now like a man possessed. While Harold was tending to his girlfriend's injuries, the 60 year old soaked a rag in petrol and threw it at his younger rival, whose clothes at once ignited. Self preservation and commonsense told Harold to get outside and to roll in the grass in order to extinguish the flames on his clothing, which by this time had engulfed much of his upper body. He was in excruciating agony as the fire burned his arms and neck. It was a terrifying sight, witnessed by several people who had been alerted by the sound of the shotgun.

Harold Martin again struggled back into the cottage, where to his horror he found the sitting room ablaze. Michelle was engulfed in flames and she was clearly in no fit state to help herself, laying halfway across the doorway leading from the hall into the sitting room. Harold was forced back by the flames and became aware of Hearne's presence in the garden. The pair began to fight.

The police and fire brigade were summoned from Carlisle and Penrith, but fortunately an off-duty fireman was passing the scene in his car and stopped to see if he could assist. He stopped the fight and had Hearne placed in a car, where he was watched by a man who had seen the whole tragedy unfold before his eyes. The fireman was then told by Harold that Michelle Page was still in the cottage. He was unable to get in to save her, the ferocity of the flames too intense for him to get through.

The police arrived and at once detained Michael Hearne, who was conveyed to Penrith police station where he remained in custody while preliminary

118

enquiries commenced in an attempt to find out exactly what had happened at Thiefside Cottage. He was remanded in custody at a special late night sitting of the Penrith magistrates, so that further evidence could be procured. Harold Martin meanwhile, was conveyed to Carlisle's Cumberland Infirmary for urgent treatment to his burns.

With the recovery of Michelle Page's body the police enquiry became a full blown murder investigation, the initial task being to identify the cause of death. Home Office pathologist Dr Edmund Tapp carried out a post-mortem. He determined that a one and a half inch shotgun wound to her abdomen would have undoubtedly proved fatal; however, he found evidence of smoke inhalation in the lungs, thus proving she was still alive on the outbreak of the blaze. He further concluded that she had actually died as a result of the burns sustained during the attack.

A forensic scientist called in as part of a team to examine the cottage and crime scene confirmed that he had found particles of clothing worn by the dead woman which had been saturated in petrol. Thus it was clear that someone had deliberately doused her clothing before starting the fire.

Michael Hearne was charged with her murder and was tried at Preston Crown Court on 27th April 1988. The court was told that Hearne had allegedly threatened to kill Michelle on two previous occasions, both since she had been seeing Harold Martin, although no physical violence had actually occurred up to the point of the incident of 1st October 1987.

In his defence, Hearne said that he was not conscious of shooting Michelle. As far as the petrol and the fire went, he had removed a full can of petrol from the boot of his car and doused the settee with it with the intention of destroying himself, not Michelle nor anyone else.

119

When he ignited the petrol he believed he must have been thrown out by the initial blast as the next thing he could recall was laying in the middle of the garden outside the blazing cottage.

He admitted that under the circumstances there was nobody else at the cottage who could have, or would have, shot her. The prosecution intimated it was not likely that he simply wanted to destroy himself in the blaze – he knew that Michelle would not return to him, and if he could not have her then no one else was going to. His intention was to destroy her. Hearne denied this suggestion.

Psychiatrists, giving their professional opinion upon his state of mind, said that he was badly affected by the loss of his factory and his descent to a life dependent upon handouts from Social Security. During some of their interviews with him he had thrown tantrums and lost his temper. It would not, they suggested, be unusual for him to lose control of his senses and commit such atrocities as he was alleged to have done on the night of 1st October 1987.

Michael Hearne's trial lasted four days before he was found guilty of murder and jailed for life. A tragic tale for all concerned, this crime brought about the destruction of three lives. At least one retains memories of his night of hell. Thiefside Cottage was looted shortly after the incident by those hungry for grisly souvenirs of the crime. Sad indeed.

Index